WALKING ON
HARRIS AND LEWIS

About the Author

Although Richard Barrett first saw the Harris Hills from Berneray in the early 1970s, he never visited the island until the spring of 2007. But having become immediately besotted, he then spent most holidays walking all parts of the islands and now lives in Màraig in North Harris, where he and his wife run a guest house.

In his working life Richard was a professional marketer with a number of multinational organisations in the UK and abroad, but still found time for recreational climbing, winter mountaineering and latterly sea kayaking. He considers the Harris Hills to be like fine wine – something that cannot be appreciated without the benefit of age and experience.

Other Cicerone guides by the author
Cycling in the Hebrides

WALKING ON
HARRIS AND LEWIS

by
Richard Barrett

2 POLICE SQUARE, MILNTHORPE, CUMBRIA LA7 7PY
www.cicerone.co.uk

© Richard Barrett 2010
First edition 2010
ISBN 978 1 85284 567 4
Reprinted 2011, 2013 (with updates)

Printed by KHL Printing, Singapore.
A catalogue record for this book is available from the British Library.
All photographs are by the author unless otherwise credited.

Acknowledgements

My thanks go to all those who knowingly or unknowingly provided information that
was invaluable in tracing routes where nothing is shown on the map, particularly those
who have contributed information to the community websites on Lewis and Harris or
the various hill-walking websites and blogs. Jonathan and his team at Cicerone were
a delight to work with and their sound guidance made delivering the manuscript and
accompanying photographs a pleasure. I also need to mention our friends David and
Jessica Platt and Nigel Green, my sisters and brothers-in-law Gillian and Nigel Broad
and Janice and Peter Tennant, as well as my wife Cindy and our children Eleanor and
Jolyon. Thank you all for your company on the routes and your patience when being
ordered about for photography. I also thank the people of Harris and Lewis for their
unfailing hospitality and universal support for this book. Harris and Lewis may be the
edge of the world, but they're the centre of mine.

Advice to Readers

While every effort is made by our authors to ensure the accuracy of guidebooks
as they go to print, changes can occur during the lifetime of an edition. If we
know of any, there will be an Updates tab on this book's page on the Cicerone
website (www.cicerone.co.uk), so please check before planning your trip. We
also advise that you check information about such things as transport, accommodation and shops locally. Even rights of way can be altered over time. We are
always grateful for information about any discrepancies between a guidebook
and the facts on the ground, sent by email to info@cicerone.co.uk or by post to
Cicerone, 2 Police Square, Milnthorpe LA7 7PY, United Kingdom.

Front cover: Harris Hills from Traigh Rosamol on the Sound of Taransay (Walk 4)

CONTENTS

LEWIS

Route symbols on OS map extracts

route

alternative route

converging routes

(🧍) start point

(🧍) finish point

(🧍) start/finish point

◀ direction of walk

For OS symbols key see OS maps.

The dunes of Tràigh Rosamol with the Harris hills behind

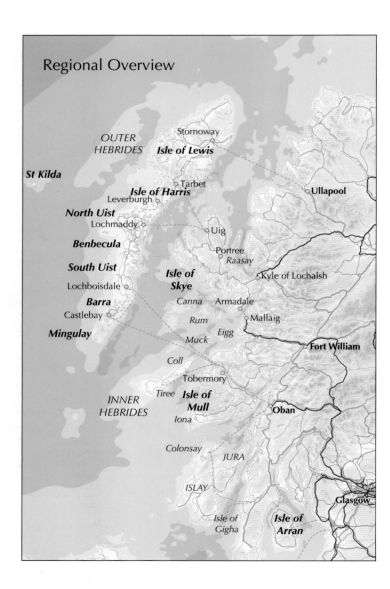

Regional Overview

St Kilda

OUTER
HEBRIDES

Isle of Lewis

Stornoway

Tarbet

Isle of Harris

Leverburgh

North Uist

Lochmaddy

Benbecula

South Uist

Lochboisdale

Barra

Castlebay

Mingulay

Uig

Portree

Raasay

Isle of Skye

Canna

Armadale

Rum

Eigg

Mallaig

Muck

Coll

Tobermory

Tiree

Isle of Mull

Iona

INNER
HEBRIDES

Colonsay

JURA

ISLAY

Isle of Gigha

Isle of Arran

Ullapool

Kyle of Lochalsh

Fort William

Oban

Glasgow

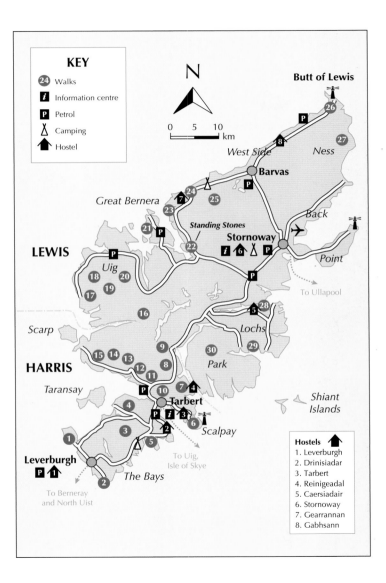

KEY

- 24 Walks
- *i* Information centre
- P Petrol
- ⚊ Camping
- ➤ Hostel

N

0 5 10
km

Butt of Lewis

Ness

P

8

West Side **Barvas**

Great Bernera

7 24
25
23

Standing Stones

21 P

22 *i* G **Stornoway**

LEWIS

Uig

18 20
17 19

P

Back

Point

To Ullapool

16

5 28

Scarp

9

30

29

HARRIS

15 14 13
12

Lochs

Park

8

11

10

7 4

P

Taransay

Tarbert

4 3 *i*

3 6

Shiant Islands

2

Scalpay

5

To Uig, Isle of Skye

Leverburgh

P 1

2

The Bays

To Berneray and North Uist

Hostels ➤

1. Leverburgh
2. Drinisiadar
3. Tarbert
4. Reinigeadal
5. Caersiadair
6. Stornoway
7. Gearrannan
8. Gabhsann

Looking south from the summit of Cleit Ard (Walk 8)

INTRODUCTION

Together Harris and Lewis make up the largest island of the 130 mile-long archipelago known as the Outer Hebrides or the Western Isles. They lie at the very edge of Europe and, other than St Kilda and a few other isolated mountain peaks rising from the ocean bed, there is nothing but ocean to the west at a latitude of 58°N until you hit the coast of Newfoundland and Labrador. During the dark winter months there are gales every third day; and the other two are simply windy! And with nothing in their way for thousands of miles, the Atlantic winds rattle ill-fitting doors and snatch carelessly pegged clothes from washing lines making the islands seem a desperate place to be.

Much of Lewis is black peat bog pitted with thousands of lochs and lochans and the interior of South Harris looks so 'lunar' that it stood in as the planet Jupiter for the filming of the sci-fi movie *2001: A Space Odyssey* back in 1968. It all makes for a seemingly unappealing and hostile place to go walking, especially when getting there will certainly take longer and could cost you more than a budget flight to the guaranteed warmth of southern Europe.

But if you're a dedicated walker, tired of the crowded hills and mountains of more accessible areas, coming to Harris and Lewis is a must. You will get solitude in abundance and won't have to go far off the few beaten

Taransay – perhaps the best known island in the Outer Hebrides after the televised 'Castaway' series

Past industry in Harris – the old whaling station at Bun Abhainn Eadarra below Mulla bho Dheas (Walk 11)

tracks to have a summit or glen to yourself. Although ferries and flights to the mainland are frequent these islands maintain an air of remoteness. Disembark at Uig after a week on the Outer Hebrides and even Skye can seem busy and boisterous, totally geared up for tourism.

In spite of being part of the same landmass, often referred to as the Long Island, Lewis and Harris are very different. With fish farming, ship building and even software development the economy of **Lewis** is much less dependent on tourism. Outside of Stornoway, the only town, the traditional occupations of crofting, fishing and weaving are still prevalent with many islanders still having more than one occupation. Having seen parents and grandparents suffering from the boom-and-bust cycles of industries such as herring fishing, weaving and rendering seaweed for chemicals, Lewis folk are proudly self-reliant and know how to get along. They also know how to enjoy themselves and although the Sabbath is still strictly observed with no shop opening or newspapers (a Sunday ferry service only started in 2009), Saturday night on the town in Stornoway is just as noisy and boisterous as in any other small town.

Harris is a total contrast; even Lewis people talk about going there as if it were another country. In many ways it is – or at least it was. In the past the mountains of Harris formed a substantial natural barrier between Lewis

and Harris, and the sea rather than road was the main means of communication and transportation. It's easy to see why, despite being part of the same landmass, they have retained the names Isle of Lewis and Isle of Harris. Everything happened at the periphery where the land meets the sea and even today there are few landlocked villages anywhere on the island. The division was more than geographic. Until 1974 it extended to local government with Lewis being part of the county of Ross and Cromarty and Harris part of the county of Inverness. Together with the other islands of the Outer Hebrides they are both now part of Comhairle nan Eilean Siar – the Western Isles Council – headquartered in Stornoway.

Compared with Lewis, Harris has far less of most things that seem to count in the modern world. It has a smaller population with barely 2000 people compared with the 18,000 in Lewis. Having little industry other than agriculture, fishing and tourism, it is far less industrialised than its neighbour. And the lack of memorials to the land struggle or the staunch resistance to Lord Leverhulme that can be found in Lewis suggests that Harris folk are perhaps more tolerant and easier going. When much of the Spanish Armada was wrecked in storms as it circumnavigated Scotland in an attempt to escape Sir Francis Drake's fleet in 1588, some of the Spanish sailors are said to have ended up on Harris. Their Mediterranean genes

SO WHAT IS AN ISLAND?

You are probably still trying to reconcile the anomaly of having the two islands of Harris and Lewis on a single landmass. But what exactly does it take to make an island? The Oxford English Dictionary defines an island as a landmass surrounded by water. This sounds straightforward. However, Hamish Haswell-Smith, renowned sailor and author of the definitive *The Scottish Islands*, was faced with the dilemma of which to include and which to omit, as listing every little skerry would result in a work that would run to many volumes. He decided to limit himself to any piece of land that is over 40 hectares at high tide and completely surrounded by seawater at low tide so that you can only get to it by getting your feet wet or by boat.

Looking down the fjord-like Loch Seaforth that divides Harris and South Lewis

Having developed a working list of 165 islands to document, map and occasionally paint with his charming watercolours, the opening of the Scalpay Bridge and the causeways that link North Uist to Berneray and South Uist to Eriskay led him to reduce his list to 162, where it has remained since. Who knows how the population on the Isle of Skye, perhaps the most famous of Scottish islands, feels about being excluded from the list? Perhaps Hamish has to use an alias whenever he anchors in Portree harbour?

are supposed to give the indigenous population a darker complexion and an easier manner than the blond, blue-eyed Lewismen, many of whose ancestors came from Norway. Who knows? It is also said that the Gaelic spoken in Harris has a softer lilt to it than that spoken in Lewis. Certainly everything else about the place seems to have a similar charm. But don't dismiss either. Harris may have higher hills and a greater number of beaches, but Lewis has more prehistory, more tourist attractions – and ultimately many more hills.

GEOLOGY

The main islands of the Outer Hebrides and the north-western part of the Scottish Highlands are made up of some of the oldest rocks in Europe,

known since the late 19th century as Lewisian gneisses. The name describes a series of metamorphic rocks formed by intense pressure and temperature over a period of 1500 million years. Most of these gneisses started off as igneous rocks, such as granites and gabbros, formed by the cooling and crystallisation of magma nearly 3000 million years ago. These original rocks were then destroyed when they were buried, reheated and subjected to great pressures in the earth's crust, eventually forming the metamorphic gneiss complexes we see today.

Lewisian gneiss is characterised by narrow, alternating bands of contrasting colours. The paler bands, which are typically pale grey or pink, are made up of crystals of quartz and feldspar, whereas the darker green and black bands are largely made

Lewisian gneiss below Sron Godamull

15

up of minerals called amphiboles. Examples of this striation can be seen in the exposed boulders on the western beaches of both Harris and Lewis as well as in many of the stones at Calanais.

Most of Lewis and the mountains of North Harris are made up of banded gneisses, but moving west and south there are increasingly more veins of hard pink granite and metamorphosed gabbro and related rocks, until at the extreme south of Harris there is a narrow band of metamorphosed sedimentary rock similar to that found at the extreme north of Lewis. Granite is less easily eroded than the surrounding gneiss and good examples can be seen in the sea stacks to the south of Uig Bay in Lewis and on the Ceapabhal promontory in the southwest corner of Harris. The coarsely crystallised pink and white granite found here is known as pegmatite and is largely made up of feldspar and quartz. It forms a distinct horizontal band across the hill that is obvious from quite a distance, especially when it catches the light. In addition to the large pink crystals of feldspar and white crystals of quartz, the rock is shot through with flakes of dark red garnet crystals and clear muscovite and glossy black biotite micas.

Since feldspar melts over a wide temperature range, depending on its composition, it is used in the manufacture of ceramics. When mixed with the clays it makes them easier to work and produces a stronger and more durable product. The peak of Roineabhal at the southern end of Harris and other outcrops around the nearby Lingreabhagh are made up of a rare type of whitish igneous rock known as anorthosite, which consists almost entirely of feldspar. During World War II a quarry at Sletteval on the north-east slopes of Roineabhal provided most of the feldspar that the UK needed to manufacture porcelain electrical insulators. However, the cost of extracting the feldspar proved to be greater than the cost of foreign imports and its colour meant that it produced inferior porcelain; therefore, as has been the plight of most commercial activity in the islands, it was a short-lived venture.

But this was not the end of quarrying in South Harris. Although small-scale quarrying restarted in the 1960s but again soon petered out, other people had ideas on a far larger scale. Starting in 1974, plans were produced to develop a coastal super-quarry to extract ten million tons of aggregates each year for 60 years, much needed, it was argued, to satisfy growing demand on mainland UK. Thirty years later in 2004, the developers eventually made a dignified retreat but by then the case had become the longest running and most complex planning case Scotland had ever seen, with more than 100 witnesses and over 400 written submissions heard during 83 days of advocacy that were part of the public inquiry. If planning permission had been granted, and once the quarry was exhausted, almost a third

16

Sron Uladail – 250m of overhanging Lewisian gneiss with the 'cnoc and lochan' terrain of Morsgail Forest in the distance (Walk 14)

of Roineabhal would have disappeared. Fortunately it is still with us and remains one of the best.

The rugged and desolate landscape of Lewis and Harris today dates from the most recent ice age that scoured away loose rock and deepened and widened pre-existing valleys, leaving the fjord-like lochs and sea lochs such as Loch Sìophort (Loch Seaforth). Many of the basins formed by the ice are now filled with either water or peat and surrounded by ice-sculpted crags. This 'cnoc and lochan' landscape is best seen in the Bays area on the east coast of Harris: *cnoc* meaning hillock, *lochan* meaning a little loch. Further north in Lewis the retreating ice laid down smooth, undulating layers of glacial rubble called till. Subsequently peat formed on top of this layer which, being rich

in clay, is poorly drained. From about 11,500 years ago, when the sea level was 50m below today's level, the dry Arctic climate was gradually replaced by a relatively warm maritime climate dominated by the Gulf Stream. As the ice withdrew back to the poles the seas rose, changing the coastline and reducing the landmass. Around 6000 years ago it was 20m below current levels and it continues to rise, the east coast region of the Bays in South Harris being typical of a recently drowned landscape.

The sheer variety of terrain and the dramatic changes within the space of a short car ride are what make Harris and Lewis so appealing. Not only is there the possibility of four seasons in one day with the weather, but there are also high hills, remote moorland, vertiginous rock faces,

Four seasons in one May morning on Oireabhal – snow, then hail followed by sun and eventually a shower (Walk 13)

deep sea lochs, silver beaches and emerald seas all in one neat package. You can rise early and enjoy a strenuous walk in the hills in the morning then chill out on a deserted beach in the afternoon sun. There are few other parts of Great Britain that can provide the same exhilarating mix, and while those seeking derring-do may only come to the island in their later years, what they will find here is much like well-aged single malt – well worth waiting for.

FLOWERS AND VEGETATION

Pollen grains preserved within the peat bogs indicate that, following the ice ages, the terrain on these islands was colonised by a pioneer community of sub-alpine herbaceous plants and low shrubs. This was followed by

heather, juniper and grass and subsequently, around 8000 years ago, by trees such as birch, hazel and oak. Large pieces of 'bogwood' are occasionally uncovered under the peat layer and indicate that Harris and Lewis once had more trees and shrub cover than they do today. This is particularly evident in Marbhig in the North Lochs area of Lewis where tree stumps are regularly unearthed.

Man's need for wood and land for cultivation together with the overgrazing caused by an overpopulation of sheep and deer are traditionally blamed for the lack of trees, but it is more complex than that. The 'natural decline' model describes a shift to a wetter, cooler climate a few thousand years ago which caused peat layers to build up, engulfing woodlands and making it increasingly difficult for seeds to germinate in the waterlogged conditions, thus reducing the amount of land suitable for trees to grow. The grazing pressure of the large populations of sheep and deer prevents trees and scrub from re-establishing themselves anywhere outside of the steep ravines and fenced-off plantations where they are found today.

About 12–15 per cent of the Scottish deer population is culled each year, providing income from commercial stalking and venison for the table. Being totally free-range and expertly dispatched in a micro-second, it could be argued that it is the perfect meat for human carnivores with concerns for animal husbandry. However, research suggests that only a sustained annual cull of around 80 per cent would restore the balance between the

vegetation and deer and allow trees once again to colonise. Where this has been practised, such as on the slopes of Creag Meagaidh in the Central Highlands, the effect on the ecology has been profound. In little more than a decade the area of woodland has spread tenfold with seedlings of birch, rowan, willow, aspen and oak, resulting in an associated increase in birdlife, flora and invertebrates and creating a biodiversity not seen for many centuries. With careful consideration for the livelihoods of those engaged in deer husbandry and stalking, the same could be achieved in parts of Harris and Lewis, and would transform the landscape.

But the islands are far from barren, with the hills, moors and beaches presenting a wide variety of

Harris Hills from Traigh Rosamol on a summer's day – but the weather can change remarkably quickly

habitats for plant life. Most plants are small and need searching out, like the delicate alpines or the 150 or so species of mosses and liverworts that occur on the rocky hillsides. But when they erupt in mass flowering the islands become spectacular, and the highlight of the year is when the machair – the 'shell meadow' behind the dunes – is carpeted with wild flowers during the summer months. Most of the plants are commonplace – ragwort, buttercup, clover, daisy, various vetches and trefoils and, in later months, rarer orchids – but collectively the effect is unforgettable. The best places to see this are on the west coasts of South Harris and the Uig area of West Lewis.

WILDLIFE

Although carrying a pair of binoculars round the neck can be uncomfortable and detract from the pleasure of a walk, they are an essential piece of kit in the Western Isles and will eventually add to the enjoyment of the day.

There is only a small number of native mammal species on the islands. Common seals can be seen on islands in sheltered inlets, particularly in the Bays area of South Harris. Grey seals tend to be more difficult to see, but come ashore in great numbers on the uninhabited island of Shillay in the Sound of Harris. Similarly, although you will often see their tracks in the sand along the

western shores, otters are elusive and are best seen either early in the morning or at twilight.

Red deer are numerous in the higher hills of North Harris, Uig and Park and if you scan the skyline you will frequently find yourself being watched by large herds of them. During the summer months they can often be seen around the high-level lochans between the summits of Huiseabhal Mòr and Oireabhal where they collect to drink in the heat of the day.

The mountain hare (*Lepus timidus*) is much more difficult to see as the local population is small and it is as secretive as its name suggests. It is also known as the blue hare and sometimes the 'varying hare' due to the changing colour of its coat across the seasons. In summer they have a greyish blue coat, and in winter they are predominantly white with only the tips of their ears remaining dark. Mountain hares moult twice a year, in late autumn and again in the spring, when they lose their winter coat. The mountain hare is smaller than the brown hare and has shorter ears and legs, but this does not compromise its speed; when threatened by a predator, such as an eagle, it can easily attain 60kph for short periods. The hares are mainly solitary and live high in the mountains, which is probably why they are a particular favourite with mountain walkers.

A large number of bird species, both native and migrant, can be seen around Harris and Lewis, and one of the best places to start is on the ferry crossing from the mainland when gannets, guillemots and shearwaters can regularly be seen. In late spring there are also puffins, especially on the crossing from Uig to Tarbert as the breeding colonies on the Shiant Islands and Eilean Glas come to sea to feed. The common seabird species of fulmar, kittiwake, shag and a range of gulls breed all around the cliffs of both Harris and Lewis and can easily be observed at close quarters at Dun Eistean and on Tolsta Head. Here there are also great and arctic skuas who may mob anyone straying too near to their nests.

Sea ducks, such as the common scoter, velvet scoter and the majestic long-tailed duck, can be seen in the sheltered bays of the west coast in early spring, a time when many inland lochs are home to a pairs of red-breasted mergansers. Many species, such as the waders that congregate on the saltings at Taobh Tuath, can be viewed from the comfort of a car. Seeing others, such as the red-necked phalarope (that only breeds on the Loch na Muilne reserve near Arnol in West Lewis) and the white-billed diver (most often found on the sea off Port Sgiogarstaigh near the Butt of Lewis in late spring) involves both a walk and a great deal of patience.

Everyone who visits Harris and Lewis wants to see a golden eagle, and outside of the breeding period, when both birds are at the nest, it is not too difficult. There were 59 breeding pairs reported on the islands in 2005 and all you really need to do is park up in hilly country, look up and wait. If it looks like an ironing board with shirt sleeves hanging off the ends floating across the sky, then it is a golden eagle. Equally magnificent is the white-tailed or sea eagle. These were originally reintroduced on the island of Rum in the Inner Hebrides in the 1970s, but quickly spread to other islands and now frequent the deserted sea lochs such as Loch Sealg in Park (Walk 30). Their ability to take lambs has not made them universally welcome in the Western Isles.

One of the big attractions of bird watching in the Western Isles is the variety of migrants passing through in spring and autumn as well as off-course vagrants that get blown in during storms. There is a small but active group of recorders on Harris and Lewis and. Visit www.thewesternisles. co.uk/birdsightings.htm to catch up with their latest sightings.

GETTING THERE

Getting to the Western Isles is a major undertaking. This, and the uncertainty of the weather, perhaps explains why there are so few tourists even in the middle of summer. The distance from London to Harris is roughly 1000km (650 miles), making it about the same as a trip to the French Alps. For most

Uisgneabhal Mòr from Àird Asaig

people, that probably means a two-day drive with an overnight stop. Going south to somewhere such as the Chamonix valley with its enticing arêtes and glaciers is also likely to cost less than heading for Lewis and Harris, where the only certainty is peat bogs and midges. The choice is yours – but once you are committed to going, getting there is an adventure in itself.

By air

Currently the following airlines have scheduled flights into Stornoway on Lewis:

- Flybe has regular services from Belfast, Birmingham, Edinburgh, Glasgow, Inverness, Kirkwall, Manchester, Southampton and Sumburgh. For further information 0871 700 2000 or www.flybe.com;
- Eastern Airways has a daily flight from Monday to Friday from Aberdeen. For further information 08703 669 100 or www.easternairways.com.

By sea

Caledonia MacBrayne operates ferries on the following routes:

- from Ullapool on the Scottish mainland into Stornoway, every day of the week – journey time 2hrs 45mins;
- from Uig on the Isle of Skye into Tarbert, Harris – journey time 1hr 40mins.

- from Berneray in North Uist into Leverburgh, Harris every day of the week – journey time 1hr. As this ferry operates on Sundays it can be linked with the Uig to Lochmaddy ferry, which also runs on Sundays, as a way of getting to and from the mainland on the Sabbath. However, it will take up most of your day.

To save the disappointment of being left on the quayside, reservations are recommended for vehicles especially during the summer months, although this is not necessary for foot passengers. Since the autumn of 2008 Road Equivalent Pricing is being tested on certain routes, where ferry fares are based on the equivalent cost of road travel. If this becomes a permanent fixture, and initial discussions to get North Harris designated as a national park come to fruition, the Outer Hebrides may become much more of a magnet for tourists. Then it may become imperative to make a reservation. For further information contact 08000 665 000 or see www.calmac.co.uk.

You will undoubtedly have to schedule your travel to coincide with ferry departure times and one of the usual ways of getting to the Outer Hebrides is to drive through the night and take an early morning ferry. With two people sharing the driving it is possible to take advantage of the relatively empty roads and make good progress, freshening up with a shower

Approaching Tarbert on the ferry from Skye

on the ferry before enjoying a full Scottish breakfast in the cafeteria. It should be borne in mind that north of the main motorway network around Glasgow and Edinburgh there are few 24hr filling stations other than Fort William and Inverness, so keep an eye on the fuel gauge.

Although Ullapool to Stornoway is by far the busiest ferry route, Uig to Tarbert is a personal favourite for a number of reasons. Travelling from the south the scenery is better, with views of Glencoe and the Cuillins on a clear day. At about 90mins, the crossing itself is just the right length with lots of interest out at sea: the Ascrib Islands in Loch Snizort as you leave Uig; the Fladdachuain off the north coast of Skye; and the Shiants as you get closer to Harris. With the help of binoculars it is possible to pick

out the house that the writer Compton Mackenzie had re-roofed during the period 1926–7 when he owned the Shiants. If that is not sufficient reason to favour this route, the fare is also a few pounds cheaper than the Ullapool to Stornaway crossing.

By rail

It is quite possible to get to Lewis and Harris by rail. Heading for Harris, the rail network terminates at Kyle of Lochalsh, but a bus service connects directly with the ferry terminal at Uig on the Isle of Skye. Likewise, if heading for Lewis, a bus service links Inverness station directly with the ferry terminal at Ullapool.

For further information, contact Scotrail on 0845 601 5929 or see www.firstgroup.com/scotrail. This service does not carry bicycles, so if you are cycling you can either take the train as far as Garve and then cycle to Ullapool or use the Highland Cycle Bus that runs from Inverness to Durness via Ullapool in the tourist season. Phone 01463 222444 or see www.decoaches.co.uk for times and bookings. For further information contact Scotrail on 0845 601 5929 or see www.firstgroup.com/scotrail.

GETTING AROUND

In your own car
There are some 320km (200 miles) of road on Lewis and Harris. Some of it, like the descent from North Harris into Tarbert, is of an exceptionally good standard. Other stretches, such as the road around the eastern Bay area of Harris, tend to be narrow and winding. Having a vehicle on the island makes getting around to the more remote parts very easy. However, the only filling stations in Harris are at Leverburgh, Tarbert and Ardhasaig and the only ones in Lewis are at Stornoway, Lower Barvas, Leurbost, Uig, Cros and Bernera, with only one in Stornoway and the one on Bernera currently open on Sundays. Fuel also costs around 10p a litre more than on the mainland.

By rented vehicle
If you arrive by air you will probably need to rent a car. There are vehicle rental companies based in Stornoway and Arnol.

Passing places – essential on the miles of single-track roads on Harris and Lewis

Stornoway	
Economy Car Hire	Tel: 07552 387598
Lewis Car Rentals	Tel: 01851 703760
MacKinnon Self Drive	Tel: 01851 702984
United Rental Group	Tel: 01851 702984
Arnol	
Arnol Motors	Tel: 01851 710548

Car and van hire is available at the airport through Stornoway Car Hire. See www.stornowaycarhire.co.uk for further information or telephone 01851 702658.

Taxis are available at the airport and the airport bus service runs at regular intervals throughout the day. Contact 01851 702256 for the latest timetables.

By bus

If you plan your itinerary well it is possible to visit the island and get around using public transport. Even if you bring your own car, you may still need to use a bus to get to the start of a linear walk. Different routes are operated by a range of operators and the service timetable changes during school holidays. The complete timetable is available online at www.cne-siar.gov.uk/travel and if you are planning to make use of them during your stay, it is probably better to print out a complete set and bring it with you. Many services begin or end at Stornoway bus station, which can be contacted at 01851 704327. Otherwise Stornoway Tourist Information Office (01851 703

088) or Harris Tourist Information Office (01859 502 011) can provide information during opening hours.

By cycle

It costs nothing to take a cycle on the ferry and it makes an ideal way to get around, especially if you are camping or hostelling. Alternatively, cycles can be hired at Alex Dan's Cycle Centre in Stornoway (01851 704 025), at Bike Hebrides in Cnip (07917 846 484) and at Harris Cycle Hire (01859 520 319) and Harris Outdoor Adventure (07788 425 157) in Leverburgh.

WHERE TO STAY

Both Lewis and Harris offer a range of hotels, guest houses, B&Bs and hostels, so there is something to suit most pockets. If you prefer self-catering accommodation there are numerous holiday homes in all parts of the islands and this may be a more economical option for larger parties.

The cheapest option is a tent and this also gives the flexibility to move around. Although the right to roam means you can camp anywhere in Scotland, if you want amenities such as toilets and showers the only choices are the sites at Stornoway and North Shawbost in Lewis and Liceasto in Harris. During the summer months mobile homes tend to congregate behind the beaches at Riof in Lewis and Hogabost in Harris where there are public toilets. The odd tent is unlikely to cause problems but expect

Gatliffe Trust bunkhouse at Gearranan Blackhouse Village (Walk 23)

to pay a fee as the sites are on communal grazing land. Otherwise there is a tap near the school at Seilbost, but no toilet facilities, and as you are in a fairly populated part of the islands it may be difficult to find the solitude required for 'rough' camping!

Accommodation is in short supply and in the peak season even campsites can get full, so it is advisable to make a reservation before you arrive on the islands. Whatever your needs, a good place to start looking for accommodation is on the Visit the Outer Hebrides website www.visitouterhebrides.co.uk.

SAFETY CONSIDERATIONS

Much of Harris and Lewis is remote and in a normal day you will encounter few fellow walkers. You are very much on your own. There is no resident mountain rescue team so even if you are able to raise the alarm it is likely to be some time before assistance arrives. Therefore preventative measures and good risk assessment are vital. In addition to normal good mountain craft, the tips below may help.

- Unless you are entirely confident in your navigation skills, think twice before venturing into the higher hills alone. Going as a pair is better, but being a party of three or more is preferable so that one person can remain with any casualty while the other raises help.

- Check the weather forecast before you set out. As the Outer Hebrides are essentially a small

27

Harris Hills from Beinn Losgantir (Walk 4)

landmass in a large maritime environment, it pays to check shipping forecasts and coastal waters forecasts as they will give you the outlook for wind speeds and visibility. These can be heard on BBC Radio 4 at 198 kHz on long wave at 0048, 0520, 1201 and 1754, accessed through the BBC Weather pages on the Web or obtained from the local tourist information offices in Tarbert and Stornoway. If you do you will lessen the risk of getting caught out in a gale or having to test your navigation skills in the mist. The wind deserves respect in the Western Isles. In January 2005 the islands experienced the worst gales for 50 years with a lorry driver in Lewis reporting a sheep being blown across his windscreen! Sadly a family of five was killed during the same storm when their car was blown off the South Ford causeway that links Benbecula and South Uist. If in doubt, put the walk off until the next day and find something else to do!

- A whistle, watch, torch, survival shelter, first-aid kit and emergency food rations are all essential when venturing into high or remote terrain.

- With a scale of 1:25,000 the Ordnance Survey Explorer series gives much more information than the 1:50,000 Landranger series and will make it easier to navigate this potentially difficult terrain. Purists will be happy to navigate with a map and compass, but having a hand-held

GPS (global positioning system) will be an added safeguard and will certainly help you move more confidently, and therefore faster, over the often bleak moorland. Whatever you chose, it pays to be diligent, frequently checking your exact location and looking backwards so as to familiarise yourself with what may become a much-needed exit route.

- Being exposed to wind and sun, the effects of which are intensified by the surrounding sea, it is always worthwhile during the summer months to include lip balm, sun hat and a high-factor suncream in your pack. Since the weather can change rapidly, and what starts out as a warm sunny day can quickly deteriorate into an unpleasant squall, it is always worth carrying a warm hat and gloves at any time of year.

- Although some of the mobile phone networks give remarkably good reception in parts of the Outer Hebrides, it would be foolhardy to rely on a mobile to raise a distress call in the mountains. It is far better to leave your itinerary and estimated time of return with someone before you set out into the hills – remembering to let them know of your safe return lest they alert the support services.

MIDGES

The peat bogs of Lewis and Harris provide the ideal breeding ground for a midge, *Culicoides impunctatus*, which despite being less than

Ceapabhal and Taransay from Losgantir

2mm long has the infinite capacity to deter people from visiting the Hebrides. The midges swarm in the early morning and evening from May through to September and, once bitten, most people come out in red itchy blotches. The odd bite is tolerable, but being feasted on by a swarm results in a mass of irritable and inflamed lumps and bumps that will take a few days to disappear. Prevention is better than cure and there is a choice of repellents ranging from natural substances such as citronella through to chemically-based creams, sprays and wipes available at pharmacies. Bumps can be treated with antihistamine creams which can also be found at the pharmacy.

There are other things you can do to minimise being bitten.

- Stay indoors in the early morning and evening and even then keep the windows closed.
- If you are camping and have little choice about being outdoors, choose a location which is not damp or shaded. Try to pitch somewhere that is sunny and subject to a steady breeze, such as on a west-facing coast or on higher ground, as a light wind tends to blow the midges away. They certainly never show during a gale – perhaps they never venture out, or perhaps they do and just get blasted across The Minch to the mainland!

- Keep arms and legs covered up with light clothing and get a hat with a midge net to protect the face and neck.
- Try the Marmite diet! Eating two pieces of bread or toast with a thick layer of Marmite for two weeks prior to your trip is reputed to make you unattractive to midges, as are additional quantities of Vitamin B1.
- If you can, stick close to those who are prone to bites in the hope that the midges will overlook you! Reputed to work – although annoyingly the hapless victims tend to keep running off.

FOOTWEAR

Lewis and much of Harris consist of peat bog and even the summit plateaus of the highest mountains can be distinctly 'quaggy'. The wet conditions underfoot might lead you to consider wearing wellingtons for walking but this would be unwise. While they might be a suitable choice for short, low-level walks, wellingtons do not provide the support needed to move safely on steep ground; neither do they have the type of sole needed for a good grip on wet rock. Today most good quality, ankle-height walking boots are totally waterproof and you will only get a wet foot if you go in up to your calf.

In the days when walkers wore knee length breeches gaiters were ubiquitous, but nowadays they are less often seen on the hills. They will

Abandoned blackhouses around Ob Leasaid in South East Harris

provide protection when moving through wet grass and heather and will certainly help keep your trousers clean, but they cannot be expected to keep your feet completely dry.

Walking in the more remote parts of the islands is inevitably going to involve fording streams; carrying a pair of chunky plastic beach shoes and a towel in your pack may be advisable, especially if you do not have overnight access to drying facilities. However, if you cannot see the bottom of a stream or if it is in spate, you should either venture upstream to find a narrower and easier place to cross or turn back.

ACCESS

In Scotland there has long been a general presumption of access to all land unless there is a very good reason for the public to be excluded. The Land Reform Act 2003 confirmed this presumption, and walkers in Scotland now have a statutory right of access to all land, except for areas such as railway land, quarries, harbours, airfields and defence land where the public are excluded by law. Access rights extend to all beaches and foreshores.

Walkers should act responsibly when exercising their right of access, and follow the Scottish Outdoor Access Code published by Scottish Natural Heritage and available at www.outdooraccess-scotland.com. For example, you should avoid walking across growing crops or croftland when there is a route round it, and obey advisory signs asking you to avoid certain areas at certain times for land management, safety or conservation reasons. Particular care should be taken during the deer-stalking season, which typically runs from 1 July to 20 October, and the grouse-shooting

An Cliseam across Loch Maraig (Walk 11)

season which runs from 12 August to 10 December. During these times it is best to check with the local tourist information offices which will be able to give you contact details for any nearby estates.

Access rights extend to wild camping; as long as you have no motorised transport, a small number of people using lightweight tents can stay for up to three or four nights in any one spot. It is therefore possible to wander off into the wilderness of the Park area of south-east Lewis, or indeed any other remote area of Harris or Lewis, and simply lose yourself. Leave no sign of ever having been there by carrying out refuse and removing all traces of your pitch. I will not dwell on the risk of open fires because finding wood on Lewis and Harris is never easy; but if you are lucky enough to find something to burn, such as old woody

heather roots, ensure that your fire is sufficiently isolated from surrounding heather so as to preclude a major fire. Uncontrolled fires burn very fiercely and can set fire to the peat in which the heather grows. Not only can these fires be very difficult to quench, but where the peat is burnt heather and other seeds are destroyed, and plant life is lost; erosion may follow and it will take many years for the ground to recover.

MAPS

The vignettes from the Ordnance Survey Landranger 1:50,000 series that are shown here are included to give readers a feel for the overall course of each walk, but they are no substitute for carrying and frequently referring to a separate map. The OS Landranger series will stand you in good stead for most of the low-level walk, but it is advisable to use the OS Explorer 1:25,000 series for any high-level walk or excursion in the more remote areas where there are few marked footpaths. They show much more detail and will be far more useful in situations when you really need them, such as when finding your way across open moorland in a mist.

The maps needed for each route are listed in the individual route profiles. Collectively they are OS Landranger Series map numbers 8, 13, 14 and 18 and OS Explorer Series map numbers 455 through to 460. You will need to buy these from a bookstore that stocks a comprehensive range of OS maps – and even then they may need to be ordered. Alternatively purchase them from an internet bookstore or directly from the Ordnance Survey online shop.

PLACE NAMES

The use of Gaelic and naming conventions on OS maps deserves a comment. Gaelic is a beautiful yet complex language. Many words, including first names and place names, are pronounced and written differently according to what word or letter precedes them or how much emphasis is put on the word. For instance, 'It is cold' is *Tha I fuar*. But 'It is very cold' becomes *Tha I glè fhuar* and the pronunciation of the last word changes. Place names are the same: *Beinn Mòr* and *Beinn Mhòr* both mean the big or high mountain, yet are pronounced differently. And just to confuse, the Gaelic word *beag* actually means little or small, and not big as English speakers might assume.

Comhairle nan Eilean Siar, the Western Isles Council, has adopted

Bhaltos in West Lewis – just one of the many place names with Norse origin

33

the pragmatic approach of labelling place names in both Gaelic and English – and even when they are not you can generally work it out for yourself. Chàrlobhagh must surely be Carloway and you can be certain that Calanais is Callanish, although it is not always so straightforward. If you have time to spare and intend to return to the north-west of Scotland, the island folk will be delighted if you take the trouble to learn a few basics in Gaelic and can start a conversation with *Ciamar a tha sibh?* (How are you?), even if you dry up after a few everyday phrases.

Many guidebooks stick firmly with the English version of place-names. To me, this smacks of linguistic imperialism. It is also not very helpful for those using the guides. Most likely you are going to be using this guide in conjunction with an Ordnance Survey map, where places and features are nearly always labelled in Gaelic, Norse or some hybrid of the two. Following that convention, I have chosen to use names taken directly from the OS maps throughout the text, making it much easier to follow route descriptions.

However, despite Ordnance Survey's laudable policy on using Gaelic or Norse places names and the lengths it goes to when updating maps, all of which can be read on the OS website, naming on OS maps is far from consistent. For instance, neighbouring lochs at NB128120 on OS Explorer series 458 are labelled

Loch Mòr Sheilabrie and *Loch Beag Sheilibridh*. There are numerous other inconsistencies, and finding such anomalies can provide yet another diversion for days when bad weather keeps you indoors.

HOW TO USE THIS GUIDE

The walks in this collection have been selected to take in most of the main summits as well as shorter, half-day walks exploring antiquities and places of interest. Each route starts with a box giving the highest point reached during the walk, the total ascent involved, the distance covered and a rough guide of the time it is likely to take. These times are based on covering 4kph on the flat with an additional allowance of an hour for each 600m of ascent. This reflects the difficulty of some of the terrain and in practice it has proved fairly near the mark. However, these timings remain an estimate and you should also take into account the fitness level of the least experienced walker in the party, the conditions underfoot and the visibility on the day. With few paths, it is remarkably easy to get lost in mist. Even with two GPSs between us my party still managed to waste an hour navigating a way off the summit of Uisgneabhal Mòr on a misty April afternoon. So if you are unaccustomed to walking in wild country, start with a low-level walk to assess your own speed over the ground before venturing into the higher hills.

HARRIS

Harris hills from Traigh Rosamul

INTRODUCTION

The hills of North Harris are the highest in the Western Isles, but none exceeds 3000ft so they are hardly a magnet for the committed Munro bagger. At 799m (2622ft) An Cliseam is the highest and the only Corbett – a Scottish peak between 2500ft (761m) and 3000ft (914m). In good weather it is a remarkably straightforward and easy approach, starting from alongside the A859 main road between Tarbert and Stornoway, which already knocks 150m off the ascent. There are three Grahams: mountains between 2000ft (610m) and 2500ft (761m)

with a drop of at least 500ft (153m) all around; in descending height they are Uisgneabhal Mòr, 729m (2390ft), Tiorga Mòr, 679m (2228ft) and Oireabhal, 662m (2170ft).

Everything else is 2000ft or less and such a modest collection of summits may lull you into thinking that days spent in the mountains of Harris are carefree and do not warrant serious planning. If anything, it is the exact opposite. Once away from the roads, the North Harris hills are a wilderness with few paths and those there are have a tendency eventually to peter out. Under foot it can

Descending the south ridge of Cleit Ard (Walk 8)

An Cliseam from Airidh a Bhruaich on the border of Harris and Lewis (Walk 11)

be boggy and there are numerous small streams to cross. After a sudden downpour these can quickly become major obstacles that can be tricky and potentially dangerous to cross. To the west are the impassable cliffs of the Atlantic coast and to the north is the difficult terrain of Lewis where endless peat bog is pitted with a maze of lochs and lochans. In addition, the weather can change dramatically in a matter of minutes. All of these factors make it an area where walkers need to pay particular attention to navigation and risk management. But it is worth it. Where else can you walk the hills surrounded by emerald seas and quite so many silver beaches?

For many years North Harris was owned by private landlords. Although the area did not suffer unduly under this arrangement, in 2003 the crofters and tenants established the North Harris Trust and secured funding to buy 58,000 acres of land and effectively become their own landlords. Since then, further funding has allowed the Trust to purchase the 7472-acre Loch Seaforth Estate. The Trust has numerous projects for the considered regeneration of North Harris, including providing low-cost housing for rent, tree planting, building a small wind farm to generate electricity for local consumption and restoring the old footpaths and drove roads. In February 2009 the majority of residents in North Harris voted to pursue National Park status which, if granted by the Scottish Parliament, will make it the third National Park to be designated in Scotland.

WALK 1
Ceapabhal and Toe Head

Start/Finish	At the road end in Northton, (NF986904)
Highest point	Ceapabhal 368m/1207ft
Climb	612m/2004ft
Distance	14km/9 miles
Time	4½ –5hrs
Map	OS Explorer 455; OS Landranger 18
Refreshments	The Temple Café in Northton opens every day including Sundays

A cursory glance at the map may suggest that this is a short, half-day route of easy walking and a modest peak. However, the climb is nearly 400m straight up from sea level and other than traversing the machair at the start and end of the walk, the going is difficult all the way. This is 'yomping' territory – either striding across knee-high heather or negotiating peat bog. However, do not be put off. The walk includes a mix of history, natural sea arches and stunning views over the Sound of Harris – and possibly out to St Kilda on a clear day. The return route looks out on to the brilliant white sands of Scarista beach and the Northton saltings which are home to many waders, including golden plover during the winter months. All of this makes the walk a miniature gem.

Rather than take up customer spaces at the café, park considerately along the road. Walk north-west to the end of the road then carry straight on along the track for 800m to a gate where paths go off in different directions. These pastures are part of the machair, a low-level coastal plain that runs along much of the Atlantic coast of the Outer Hebrides. It is formed by the wind blowing fine sand that is high in shell content onto the boggier acidic grasslands. This results in a rich fertile pasture able to support livestock and a multitude of wild flowers which

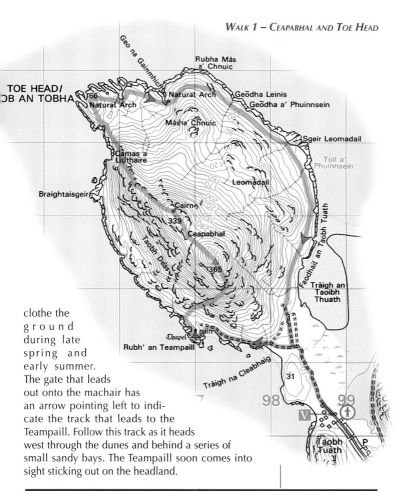

clothe the ground during late spring and early summer. The gate that leads out onto the machair has an arrow pointing left to indicate the track that leads to the Teampaill. Follow this track as it heads west through the dunes and behind a series of small sandy bays. The Teampaill soon comes into sight sticking out on the headland.

TEAMPAILL

Standing beside the remains of an older dun, which probably provided much of the materials, the present Teampaill or chapel dates from 1528 when it was built by Alasdair Crotach, Chief of the MacLeods in the same year that

39

he built the church at Roghadal. The roof would have been thatched with reeds from the nearby stream and the interior whitewashed with lime-rich shell sand. Being accessible for those living on the rich western coastal machair and the then populous islands of Pabbay and Berneray to the south, it served as the parish church for the whole of Harris before falling into disuse in the early 16th century.

There is no obvious path to the summit of Ceapabhal and any ascent is going to be arduous. Follow the coast line to the west to a stile across a stone wall. Cross this and then strike out up the hill following a band of pinkish rock that rises left to right across the hillside. This is hard going and anyone who is not a trained athlete will need frequent rests to recover their breath. ◀

It is best just to take it slowly and enjoy the view over the islands in the Sound of Harris and hills of North Uist beyond.

Following this rock band leads around to the main ridge and eventually to easier ground that leads directly to the summit of **Ceapabhal**, which means 'the bow-shaped hill' in Norse. There is a trig point and a cairn marks the summit a few metres to the north. At 368m this is a modest hill, but the views are memorable. Taransay and the

East ridge of Ceapabhal

Ceapabhal from Tràigh Huisinis

white sands of Tràigh Losgaintir and the other beaches of South Harris lie to the north-east; the now uninhabited islands of Ensay, Killegray and Pabbay and a multitude of smaller islets are scattered across the Sound of Harris to the south with Berneray and North Uist beyond. Four kilometres offshore just to the west of Pabbay lies the small island of Siolaigh, a haul-out ground for Atlantic seals. If it is particularly clear look for the Cuillin of Skye, 80km to the south-east, and the island of St Kilda, 72km away to the west.

Head off north-west to cross a boggy bealach (Gaelic for pass or col) and gain a second cairned summit marked with a spot height of 339m. Continue heading north-west, keeping to the drier and easier walking along the ridge on the left until you reach the flatter ground at **Toe Head**. The return route takes you clockwise along the coast and if you want a diversion, you could visit the natural sea arches around the headland. ▸

Unless it has been dry for some time, the going can be quaggy all the way until **Sgeir Leomadail**. The word 'quaggy' probably describes much of the low-level

There are four sea arches in total, but only two are marked on the Landranger series of maps.

41

terrain of Harris and Lewis better than any other. The word 'boggy' suggests that you run the risk of getting your feet and lower legs plastered in mud or black peat and in certain areas this can undoubtedly happen. But for the most part, the underlying layers of peat and moss mean that the ground is just springy and yielding (quaggy). It is best to move fast across such terrain, because if you stand still for too long, you are sure to sink into it and get a wet foot. But the views of the Harris Hills and the prospect of wildlife more than compensate for the possibility of a sodden sock.

Eventually the heather and peat bog gives way to pasture and walking becomes easier. A gate in a wire fence marks the first sign of a path that leads out across the fields above the sands and back to the starting point. Sgarasta across the bay was the childhood home of Finlay J MacDonald who wrote about family life there in the 1930s in his trilogy of books *Crowdie and Cream, Crotal and White* and *The Corncrake and the Lysander*. From May to September the children of the village went barefoot, and on reaching the lush pasture of the machair you might wish to treat your feet and do the same.

WILLIAM MACGILLIVRAY (1796–1852)

Now recognised as a founding ornithologist and a fine bird illustrator in his own right, during his lifetime William MacGillivray was more famous for providing the narrative that accompanied John Audubon's famous *The Birds of America*.

MacGillivray had a hard life. He was illegitimate; his father – an Aberdeen-educated army surgeon from Inverness – was killed in the Napoleonic Wars, and at the age of three young William was sent to live with his uncle Roderick at Northton. He received a remarkable education at the school at Obbe, since renamed Leverburgh, where he learned Latin and Greek. But when he wasn't deep into his books, he was engrossed in the wildlife of South Harris.

Following in his father's footsteps, he too went to university in Aberdeen, walking the 180-mile journey back to Harris for the longer vacations. His fascination with natural history inspired him to want to see the collections of the British Museum, so in 1819 he set out and walked there too, covering a wandering route of more than 800 miles in less than two months. On the way he kept records of everything of interest and drew unfamiliar plants in his notebooks, but he only stayed a week before returning to Aberdeen by sea.

He returned to Northton in the summer of 1820 and married a local girl, Marion McCaskill, before returning to Edinburgh to become Conservator to the Royal College of Surgeons. He was a prodigious writer, illustrator and natural historian, perpetually busy but never achieving the commercial success required to keep his large family. He died in 1852 having spent his final years as the Regius Professor of Civil and Natural History at Aberdeen. Many of his illustrations are now in a collection at the Natural History Museum in London.

The ways of the early natural historians, such as MacGillivray, may not fit with our modern ideas of conservation and ecology, as much of their research involved killing things and cutting them up. In his *Descriptions of the Rapacious Birds of Great Britain* published in 1836, MacGillivray remembers a boyhood adventure on Ceapabhal when he used a live white hen as bait to entice a golden eagle into the firing range of his bird hide. 'I fired, and received a serious contusion on the check, the gun having been overcharged. Impatient to know the result, I raised the roof on my back, forced myself through it, and running up to the place found the eagle quite dead, the whole shot having entered its side. So this is all, I thought, an eagle is nothing wonderful at all.' Not yet a naturalist, he had no use for the bird and it was allowed to rot on the dung heap. The hen fared better; he records that it lived to rear a brood of chickens.

WALK 2

Roineabhal from Roghadal

Start/Finish	Park alongside the wall of Roghadal Church (NG047832)
Highest point	Roineabhal 460m/1509ft
Climb	490m/1600ft
Distance	8km/5 miles
Time	3–3½hrs
Map	OS Explorer 455; OS Landranger 18
Refreshments	The Rodel Hotel, 048829; best to check if it is open in winter months. Tel: 01859 520210

Its rock-strewn slopes do not make Roineabhal an enticing hill to climb, and even on a fine summer's day you may find you have the summit to yourself. In Old Norse, Roineabhal means 'rough hill' and it is entirely appropriate. However do not be deterred, as the views make the climb worthwhile and there is the added bonus of numerous, delicate wild flowers underfoot at the right time of year.

Although there are no footpaths to the summit marked on the map, the usual ascent from Roghadal goes along the northern shore of Loch Thoragearraidh and then follows the upper reaches of Abhainn Thorrb to the summit. This route ascends the eastern ridge of Beinn na h-Aire and uses the more direct route as the descent to form a circular walk.

From the church follow the minor road north out of Roghadal towards Lingreabhagh, past the radio mast and Loch na Cachlaidh to the top of a small hill just before an unnamed steam. There is a spot height for 63m marked on the OS Explorer series at this point. Leave the road and head directly for the skyline, heading for the lowest point in the ridge to the north of the cairn at the lower, southern summit of Beinn na h-Aire, 'the hill of the lookout'. The lower part of the slope can be wet, but as you gain height

it becomes much drier, especially if you stick to the rocky slabs and boulders. Pick

your own route, and as long as you are gaining height and heading for the ridge it doesn't much matter where you go. Height is gained quickly with good views along the townships of the Bays to the north and across The Minch to Skye in the east. But don't ignore what is beneath your feet. This ascent is much like climbing through a rockery with many delicate wild flowers nestling between the boulders. ▶

Approaching the saddle the incline eases and it is time to head for the higher, northern summit of **Beinn na h-Aire** with its prominent cairn. On a clear day there are good views south over the multitude of skerries in the

In early summer there are violets, varieties of orchid and mosses and lichens in profusion.

45

Leverburgh from Roineabhal

South of Harris to the hills of North and South Uist. A small cairn marks the way to the bealach and across the top of **Coire Roineabeal**, where there is a small cairned buttress that is an irresistible spot to be photographed with the bowl of the coire and the expanse of the Bays as a backdrop. The eastern flank of the coire that leads to the northern summit of Beinn na h-Aire makes a good but loose scramble for anyone wanting a more challenging route to the summit, but it would involve walking further along the road before turning west toward Tora Cleit.

The summit of **Roineabhal** has a trig point surrounded by moss-lined stone walling and two other cairns that look south to the green fields of Roghadal and west to the watery township of Leverburgh. It is a place to linger, perhaps tracking the little ferry as it navigates a tricky passage through the shallow waters of the Sound of Harris on its way back and forth between Leverburgh and Berneray. A return journey as a foot passenger makes an enjoyable day trip, particularly on a Sunday when, other than hotel restaurants, almost everything else on Harris is shut.

When you are ready to go, head south below the rocky slopes of Beinn na h'Aire, occasionally passing the small cairns that mark the usual ascent route. Resist dropping down to the valley floor too quickly and stick to the easier ground immediately below the rocks of **Mallach na Stùdhadh** for a while before descending to pick up a grass path along the north shore of **Loch Thorsageàrraidh**. A number of indefinite footpaths criss-cross the area between the southern end of the loch and the road but, if in doubt, just head through the gorse bushes towards the church tower.

ROGHADAL

Roghadal from above Loch Thorsageàrraidh

The hotel, quay and outbuildings were built by Captain Alexander MacLeod in 1779. At the age of 70 he purchased Harris for £15,000, using a fortune he amassed as the captain of the East Indiaman clipper, *The Lord Mansfield*. As a resident landlord, MacLeod set about establishing a viable fishing industry, building fishing stations along the east coast of the Bays and the infrastructure needed to support the initiative at Roghadal, including a school and a public house. In 1786 the newly formed British Society of Extending the Fisheries commissioned a survey to explore the potential for fishing in the Hebrides and the report about Roghadal was so impressive that the Society set up fishing stations at Oban, Tobermory and Ullapool.

These flourished while the herring were populous, and have since become the major tourist locations and ferry ports of the west coast. However, Roghadal fared less well. The Customs and Excise authorities at Stornoway insisted that any cargo of salt bound for Roghadal was first unloaded there and measured for taxation purposes, having then to be reloaded and shipped down the coast to its final destination. The cost of doing this and the unpredictability of herring, which some years simply failed to show in The Minch, put paid to MacLeod's plans. Today the basin at Roghadal remains a safe harbour for passing yachts and MacLeod's house is a hotel.

ST CLEMENT'S ROGHADAL

Roghadal was the traditional burial place of the chiefs of the MacLeods of Dunvegan and it is thought that Alasdair Crotach ('Hunchback') MacLeod, the 8th clan chief, was responsible for the current building which dates from the first part of the 16th century. With its tower set on a rock outcrop, the building is certainly imposing. But it is the interior that is the real jewel, with a number of wall tombs and grave slabs judged to be the finest late-medieval sculptures to survive in the Western Isles. The intricate carvings depict a mixture of religious themes and scenes reflecting the status of those they commemorate. Naturally, the finest is the one Alasdair Crotach had carved for himself, which the inscription says was completed in 1528, well in advance of his death 19 years later. It may be that being deformed and possibly in pain for much of his life, he built his tomb in readiness for a promised salvation in the next world. He received his injury during a skirmish with the MacDonalds of Eigg when they raided the MacLeod lands on Skye in the 1480s and it must have affected him as it is said that nine of the daughters of Cameron of Lochiel refused his proposal of marriage before the 10th daughter accepted him!

However, he was still capable of wit and humour. There is a story about him dining with King James V of Scotland in the Royal Palace where he was repeatedly taunted by some English nobles who wanted to know whether a heathen Highlander had ever seen such a large hall, grand table or magnificent candelabra. Crotach silently endured the taunts, before replying that in Skye he had more marvellous candelabra, a bigger table and a far more spectacular ceiling. When the noblemen eventually came to visit him on

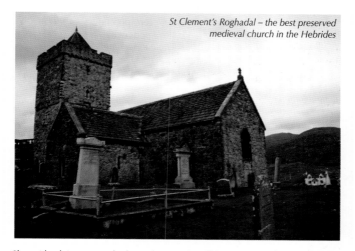

St Clement's Roghadal – the best preserved medieval church in the Hebrides

Skye, Alasdair prepared a huge feast and got his servants to lay it out on the flat summits of Healabhal Mhor and Healabhal Bheag, where they dined underneath the stars. Alasdair made his point and the mountains have been called MacLeod's Tables ever since.

While the tombs are undoubtedly the main attraction at Roghdal, there are others. Most guidebooks fail to point out the lewd panels set into the tower that depict a man and woman exposing their genitalia. It is said that they were purposefully disfigured by prudish Victorians blasting them with shot, but they still leave little to the imagination. These carvings are not simply the work of a wayward craftsman, but are *Sheela-na-gig,* examples of which can be found on early churches right across Europe. There are various theories about their purpose: they may have been put there to warn parishioners about immorality; they might have been fertility symbols or perhaps they were supposed to distract any evil that might appear while the faithful were at prayer.

Another interesting feature is an ornate cast-iron headstone in the north-east corner of the graveyard. Probably mass-produced in a Glasgow foundry with the inscribed stone plaque added by a local mason, it commemorates the death of Margaret McRae who died in childbirth in 1867.

WALK 3

Coast to Coast on the Coffin Route

Start/Finish	Road junction at the head of Loch Stocanais (NG127929)
Highest point	Bealach Eòrabhat 85m/278ft
Distance	14 km/8¾ miles
Climb	336m/1092ft
Time	4½hrs
Map	OS Explorer 455; OS Landranger 14
Refreshments	The Skoon Art Café in Geocrab and the café at Art Hebrides in Seilebost are both worth a short detour

The crossing of South Harris is a walk of extremes: from the wild barren rock of the east to the fertile machair and white sands of the west; from acid to alkaline; from the hard life endured by those displaced during the clearances of the 19th century to the easy living of the holiday homes and luxury guest houses of today. This route also marks the transition from life to death as this is the path once used by funeral parties to carry their dead to be interred in the deep soils of the west coast. So tie the lightest member of your party to a plank and re-enact a grim scene of Hebridean history!

The start of the Coffin Route is marked by a sign at the T-junction at the head of **Loch Stocanais** where there is good parking. The first few metres of the route are on a hard surface but it soon reverts to grass as it passes a sheep fank (a set of stone-walled pens used for sorting sheep) and will quickly deteriorate further into a peaty mush. The first half of the route is way-marked with poles and these will take you left below **Cnoc Biorach** and past the house at **Ceann a Bhàigh** before turning north-west and heading directly for **Bealach Eòrabhat**. As you ascend to the pass you will no doubt be asking yourself how the funeral party ever managed to carry a coffin over this quagmire. ▶ The path has been improved with drainage channels and infill and as it gains height it gets drier underfoot until at the pass it is fairly easy going. To the south of Bealach Eòrabhat is Creag an Eoin which means the 'rock of the bird' and you may be lucky enough to see one – an eagle.

Just before the path descends to the west, there are two benches where you can stop and enjoy the view across Tràigh Losgaintir to Taransay. The gravelled track to

At times you will find yourself walking like Groucho Marx with your centre of gravity being dragged down as you haul your trailing leg free of the black peat.

51

Those who remember their school geography will recognise the drumlins en echelon just below the loch.

Loch Carran is mercifully dry and the ground is covered quickly. ◄ At this point the route turns right and follows the old coast road north to the current main road which is followed east to where it crosses **Abhainn Lacasdail**. Using the old road again follow it south-east past the cottages at **Loch Lacasdail** and uphill beneath **Stocleit an Ear**. Shortly after passing a mast which is as yet unmarked on both series of OS map, the route goes through a working quarry. Proceed with care and read the instructions set out on the danger signs; if the siren can be heard, wait until the all clear is given before going any further.

Once back on the main A859 road, continue south-east towards the junction signposted for Geocrab, making use of the old road on the right as a short-cut at the junction. The babbling of the Abhainn Lackalee makes a pleasant accompaniment for the 2km walk along the road back to the start. Just before the road crosses the

Harris Hills from Losgantir

stream, look out for numerous stone walls and piers that have been built into the river along the way, thought to be for controlling the flow that worked a mill that once stood at the bottom of the hill.

THE BAYS

During the clearances of the 19th century those families who chose not to emigrate were displaced to the barren rock of the east coast, leaving the rich grazing of the western machair for the sheep. They would have traipsed across to the Bays carrying their few belongings including the scarce lengths of timber that would be essential for supporting the roof of the new black-house they would need to build. There are reports of landlords' Factors going out of their way to ensure that these essential timbers were burnt when they set fire to the evacuees' old house. As if life wasn't difficult enough?

But rather than perish, these hardy people flourished, fishing both the sea and the many trout lochs of the hinterland and building up layers of peat and seaweed to create lazybeds to grow potatoes and oats. Today there is a small township at the head of almost every inlet and many people are still involved in inshore fishing, fish farming and occasionally knitting or weaving. Over the years they have been joined by a growing number of artists and crafts people making the Bays the creative corner of Harris.

Before the arrival of metalled roads, the only way to travel between the small townships was by boat or path. The relative paucity of footpaths shown on OS maps today suggests that there were few, and those that were there eventually became the handful of arterial roads that branch off the main A859. The isolated townships of the Bays were first linked by road in the 1930s. Because it was so expensive to build, this narrow and twisting road rapidly attracted the name the 'Golden Road' – something that has stuck to it ever since. A drive along it may not provide the fine Atlantic views and sandy beaches of Harris's west coast, but in many ways the Golden Road has more to offer. The townships are charming with dwellings tucked snugly away from the worst of the winter gales. The artists' studios and galleries provide a welcome break and a chance to browse and purchase, and the many roadside lochs and lochans afford the opportunity to watch wildlife from the comfort of your car. Seals can usually be seen basking on the small islands in Loch Fhionnsabhaigh and red-breasted mergansers are numerous on the inland lochs.

Scrambling that can easily be avoided below Sron Godamuil

WALK 4
Beinn Dhubh

Start/Finish	At the kissing gate, just over the bridge that spans the Allt Tobhtan ic Fannan on the road to Losgaintir (NG095974)
Highest point	Beinn Dhubh 506m/1660ft
Climb	606m/2000ft
Distance	11km/7 miles
Time	4–4½hrs
Map	OS Explorer 455; OS Landranger 14
Refreshments	The café at Art Hebrides in Seilebost is close to the Start/Finish

It is easy to dismiss Beinn Dhubh and its neighbours as characterless hills of little merit. However their position makes them very special. On a clear day there are good views of the Harris Hills to the north, the sparkling sandy beaches of west Harris to the south and Taransay, and perhaps even St Kilda, to the west. There is no finer viewpoint on the island and it is an easy and enjoyable walk. The circular route described here takes in the main summits of Beinn Dhubh and Beinn Losgaintir and the irresistible sands of Tràigh Rosamol, unfolding in a series of rewarding views as you gain height and reach the ridge. An alternative route that takes in more of the ridge and uses a bus to return to the start is also described.

Go through the kissing gate, cross Allt Tobhtan Mhic Phannain using the stepping stones and head up through the rocky slabs to the cairn that marks the summit of **Sron Godamuil**. If you are confident moving over rock then you will enjoy linking the slabs to provide an easy, but discontinuous, scramble. If not, then keep to the grass and weave your way through the slabs. Beyond the unnamed lochan behind the cairn, the ground becomes easier and the ridge and then the summit of **Beinn Losgaintir** are soon reached, providing a whole panorama of the hills of

North Harris. Head down to a second unnamed lochan in the bealach and climb the slopes to the walled trig point that marks the summit of **Beinn Dhubh**. On a good day this is an excellent spot to enjoy a long and lazy lunch.

Having finally soaked up the view, descend to the west, passing through a gate in the fence that runs along Abhainn Aird Groadnish and a second gate in the wall above **Tràigh Rosamol**. After a paddle, or perhaps an invigorating dip, head back along the road to the start. ◄

At the end of a good summer's day the sunsets over the Sound of Taransay can be stunning.

To make a longer walk that covers more of the ridge start at Tarbert, walk along the road to Ceann Dibig (NG144980) then cross the rough ground to ascend the easier slopes of Beinn nan Leac and follow the ridge all the way to Beinn Losgaintir. Descend to the settlement of Losgaintir and follow the minor road back to the bus stop at the junction with the main A859 at NG096971.

An interesting **low-level route** for a dull day is provided by a footpath, unmarked on any OS map, which follows the coast westwards from West Loch Tarbert to Bitheasdail (NB112004). This path goes below Cnoc na Cloiche and the north face of Uamascleit and includes some difficult rock steps before reaching the impressive corrie at Bitheasdail. It could also form part of an ascent of Beinn Dubh, although the ascent out of Bitheasdail to the summit of Tothan Cartach is steep and needs care.

Looking out over Taransay from Sron Godamuil

WALK 5

The Scholars' Path

Start/Finish	Near Lochan nan Craobhag (NG146936) on the minor road that joins Greosabhagh to the A859. Park at the cattle grid (149934) just south of Lochan nan Craobhag, keeping the gate clear
Highest point	Grosa Cleit 183m/600ft
Climb	316m/1035ft
Distance	9km/5.6 miles
Time	2–3hrs
Map	OS Explorer 455; OS Landranger 14
Refreshments	Any of the cafés or hotels in Tarbert or the Skoon Art café in Geocrab

The 20-mile long Frith-Rathad na Hearadh – the Harris Walkway – consists of old paths and quieter stretches of road that have been way-marked by Harris Development Ltd to link Scaladal in North Harris to the machair at Seilebost. Parts of the Walkway are included in walks 3 and 7, but some of the best sections are to the south of Greosabhagh, down the western shore of Loch Mhic Neacail and over the ridge of Carnan Mòr, where the route follows a volcanic dyke of brown gritty rock inland behind the crofts at Leac a Li, eventually joining the road near Uamh Ard. It is barely discernable from the swirls of contours on the OS Explorer Series, but well marked on less-detailed Landranger series.

Before the 'Golden Road' was built to link the scattered township of the Bays, children used this path to get to school at Greosabhagh and later at Caolas Stocinis when a school was built there, and this section of the Walkway is sometimes called 'The Scholar's Way'. For much of its length the path is still in good repair and clearly a lot of work went into its construction and maintenance, which was the responsibility of the parish councils aided by grants from the magnificently named 'Congested Districts Board'. This suggests that in the 19th century the population of the area was much

Heading down towards Caolas Stocinis

greater than the figure that the land could be considered to support. Even today, many years after the path was last used by schoolchildren, it is still well-drained and for the most part makes pleasant and easy walking.

By making use of the very frequent bus services, it is possible to follow the Walkway all the way from Tarbert to Leac a Li, but this route includes an ascent to the modest summit of Grosa Cleit to make a shorter, circular walk.

Walk up the road and pick your own way up the eastern ridge of **Grosa Cleit** to the trig point that marks the summit. It may be a modest hill, but it is the highest in this part of the Bays and gives good views all around – north to the Harris hills, eastwards to Skye, south to Roineabhal and you can even catch of glimpse of Taransay to the west.

Descend to the west, picking a way through the rocky slabs and down to visit the remains of the shieling marked on the OS Explorer series at 138937. It is set in an oasis of green grass that would shame many suburban lawns so it is easy to

The old chapel above Caolas Stocinis

spot, which is more than can be said for Airigh Iain Oig (137934). You will do well to find anything that looks like a group of ruined shieling here! Cross the ground to the south of the eponymously named **Loch Airigh Iain Oig** to gain the road that runs down to Aird Mhighe.

There are some stone walls in the flow of Abhainn Lackalee on the right-hand side of the road at 132933 suggesting that there was once a millwheel here. A few paces further down where the stream flows under the road there is an ancient packhorse bridge that is now buried by the more recent embankment, but it is still visible if you drop down to the river bank. Another few paces and you pick up the Harris Walkway, which is marked with a faded sign set in a cairn on the left.

Go up the hill and through the first of many gates to pick up the yellow-topped marker posts and follow them alongside the fence. In a number of places sections of the path have simply sunk into the ground and there are a few wet bits that need jumping across or walking round.

As the path starts to drop towards **Caolas Stocinis** there is the roofless shell of a small stone hut on the right. This structure is distinctly odd with a very low door and small window. Might it have been built as a shelter for schoolchildren during bad weather? Go through another gate and an obvious gap in a stone wall and follow the path through a rocky gully. One the right is the roofless remains of a blackhouse. At the end of the gully on a flat area of ground on the left is a large derelict chapel. Although it can provide shelter from a downpour it is not pleasant; the floor is scattered with both the bones of dead sheep and the droppings of live sheep. A winter storm may also cause the roof to cave in, so enter at your own peril.

Continue to a metal gate above Caolas Stocinis and turn sharp left up the clearly defined path, passing through another two gates. The path now snakes and curls its way across the slopes of **Carnan Mòr** with glorious sweeps. It is level, well-drained and makes for good walking, a tribute to the men who built it. Just above **Loch Mhic Neacail** there is a bench that gives a good view along the loch where red-breasted mergansers can be found. There is another stone bridge followed by a wooden footbridge and fairly soon the path descends to Greosabhagh, a township that is memorable for the number of abandoned vehicles and waste plastic. As it is the home one of Harris's bus operators and haulage operators, the former is perhaps forgivable. Anyone looking for hand-knitted knitware or tweed should make the short diversion to visit the Isle of Harris Knitwear Company. Otherwise walk back up the road to the starting point.

WALK 6
Scalpay

Start/Finish	Park in the gravelled lay-bys north of three houses on the bend in the minor road between Port na Geiltan and the main village (NG220968)
Highest point	Beinn Scorabhaig (104m/340ft)
Climb	286m/936ft
Distance	9.5km/6 miles
Time	3hrs
Map	OS Explorer 455; OS Landranger 14
Refreshments	There is a small café at the community shop near the pier

Scalpay is riddled with sea lochs, many of which face into East Loch Tarbert and have right-angle turns in them. This makes them very sheltered moorings for the numerous small boats whose crews earn their living today fishing for shellfish. This business has been so successful and lucrative that the people of Harris are said to refer to Scalpay as 'Treasure Island'. Compared with Harris, it certainly looks and feels a busy and industrious place and despite its size supports a population of over 300 people. But get away from the main centres of population on the south-west of the island and it feels just as wild as anywhere else.

Walk south to the corner and the group of three houses. Although the route is promoted as the Scalpay Heritage Trail and is well marked throughout its length with yellow-topped posts, there is nothing to indicate the start. But it is here, and if you look to the right below the low cliff you can see it.

To reach it go through the gate that leads to the furthermost house, turn right immediately before it and pass through another gate and you're out on the moor. This good gravelled track takes you to **Loch an Dùin** where there are the remains of a dun, once reached by a causeway that was submerged when the outflow to the loch was dammed to raise the water level. Go left, crossing a stile and a footbridge to reach the first marker pole. It is now just a matter of following them down the length of the island. However, the route is very wet and you may wish to retreat to the higher ridges in search of drier ground.

At the end of the loch the route passes through a gate then turns along the south side of **Loch Cuilceach**, before climbing up to the twin cairns at the summit of **Beinn Scorabhaig**. The views north to the empty Pairc area of South East Lewis and the Shiant Islands out at sea are well worth the exertion and the sodden feet. From here you can also see **Eilean Glas lighthouse** below and the route sweeps round a group of unnamed lochs towards it. ▶ Turn right and follow the wall to a gate, which leads directly to it.

The lighthouse is surrounded by a fine stone wall, which was built to provide shelter for the crops that the keepers grew in order to be self-sufficient in this remote spot.

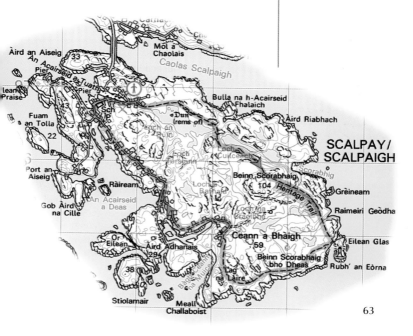

63

The lighthouse on Eilean Glas

Not only was **Eilean Glas lighthouse** the first in the Outer Hebrides, it was the first on the whole west coast of Scotland. It was built between 1787 and 1789 by Thomas Smith, father-in-law of Robert Stevenson, the first of the famous Stevenson dynasty of lighthouse builders who were responsible for the later addition of the tower and the keepers' accommodation. During late spring and the summer months puffins can be seen along the top of the cliffs. However, birdlife did not always have it so good at Eilean Glas; the last great auk recorded in Scotland was captured here in 1821.

Return through the gate, turn left along the wall and follow the marker posts southwest down to **Lag na Laire**. Continue following the posts northwards to reach the road at **Ceann a Bhàigh**. The 3km walk back to the start provides continual interest. There are distant views of the hills of North Uist and plenty to keep you occupied nearer to hand with deserted crofts, lazybeds, boats and a number of yappy dogs that seem to send the alarm from house to house. After a longish stretch alongside An

Acairseid a Deas (South Harbour) the road leads to the busy village scattered around An Acairseid a Tuath (North Harbour). Turn right at the bridge at Ceann a Bhàigh (218967) to return to the start.

In 1998 Prime Minister Tony Blair formally opened the £6.4m **Scalpay Bridge**, which replaced the ferry that had previously shuttled back-and-forth across Caolas Scalpaigh. Not only was it a significant event for Scalpay and Harris, helping to secure investment and jobs at the new seafood processing plant, but also it was the fist time that a serving prime minister had ever been to the Outer Hebrides. One unanticipated effect of the new bridge is the impact on human interaction. Scalpay residents used to make the most of the frequent waits for the ferry to chat with the ferryman and other island dwellers and share their family news. Now they simply wave to each other from the isolation of their vehicles as they pass on the bridge.

Scalpay Bridge

WALK 7

Circuit of Tòdun from Urgha

Start/Finish	At the car park at the southern end of Lochannan Lacasdail, 2.5km east of Tarbert on the road to Scalpay (NB183004)
Highest point	Tòdun 528m/1732ft
Climb	1029m/3370ft
Distance	19km/12 miles
Time	6hrs
Map	OS Explorer 456; OS Landranger 14
Refreshments	Various cafés and hotels in Tarbert

This route uses some very old footpaths that link the remote townships of Reinigeadal, Molingeanais and Màraig with Tarbert. If you wish you can miss out Molingeanais, which saves 2.5km and the best part of an hour but it is well worth a visit. At its peak in the 1880s Molingeanais supported a population of around 40 and a school was built there in 1921. In 1935 the authorities withdrew the teacher, which effectively closed the school, and paid a lodging allowance for the children to go to Tarbert. This meant that, together with the children from Reinigeadal, they had to traipse backwards and forwards each week along the path that makes up the first part of this route. This must have been an arduous travail in a winter gale as the path reaches a height of 280m at the bealach between Trolamul and Beinn Tharsuinn. The last residents left Molingeanais in the 1960s and the village stands deserted. Reinigeadal fared better; a tarmac road was eventually pushed through in 1989 giving Reinigeadal the claim to be the most recent coastal village to be connected into the road network anywhere in the UK. Today there is a small but growing community and a remote hostel run by the Gatliff Hebridean Hostels Trust.

The walk offers some fine views out to the Shiant Islands and down the fjord-like Loch Seaforth that splits North Harris from the Pairc district of Lewis. Without access to a boat or a readiness for a wilderness expedition starting from Eisken in the north, this area is inaccessible. Even so, in the

1820s there were 36 townships there, all of which were cleared for sheep and latterly deer.

Leaving the road at the southern end of **Lochannan Lacasdail**, follow the well-defined footpath signposted for the Gatcliff Youth Hostel at Reinigeadal as it climbs up eastwards across the moor. After passing the cairn that marks the bealach between Trolamul and Beinn Tharsuinn the path starts to descend above the left bank of **Gill Garbh**. A smaller path crosses the stream and forks off down to the now deserted village of Molingeanais. Ignore this if you are doing the shorter route and continue along the main path as it zigzags dramatically down steep ground to reach a footbridge at the head of Loch Trolamaraig.

If you are including **Molingeanais**, take the smaller path which leads directly down to the village. In late summer this path is a delight, being fringed with heather as it gently drops down to the coast. Some of the houses at Molingeanais have been restored as holiday retreats, so on reaching the boundary fence be sure to respect the privacy of any residents who may be there. The name Molingeanais comes from *moll* meaning shingly beach and *innis* meaning green pasture, so it is not by chance that both these features are to be found here, and the

Tòdun from above Molingeanais – a more recently deserted village in Harris now being brought back into use

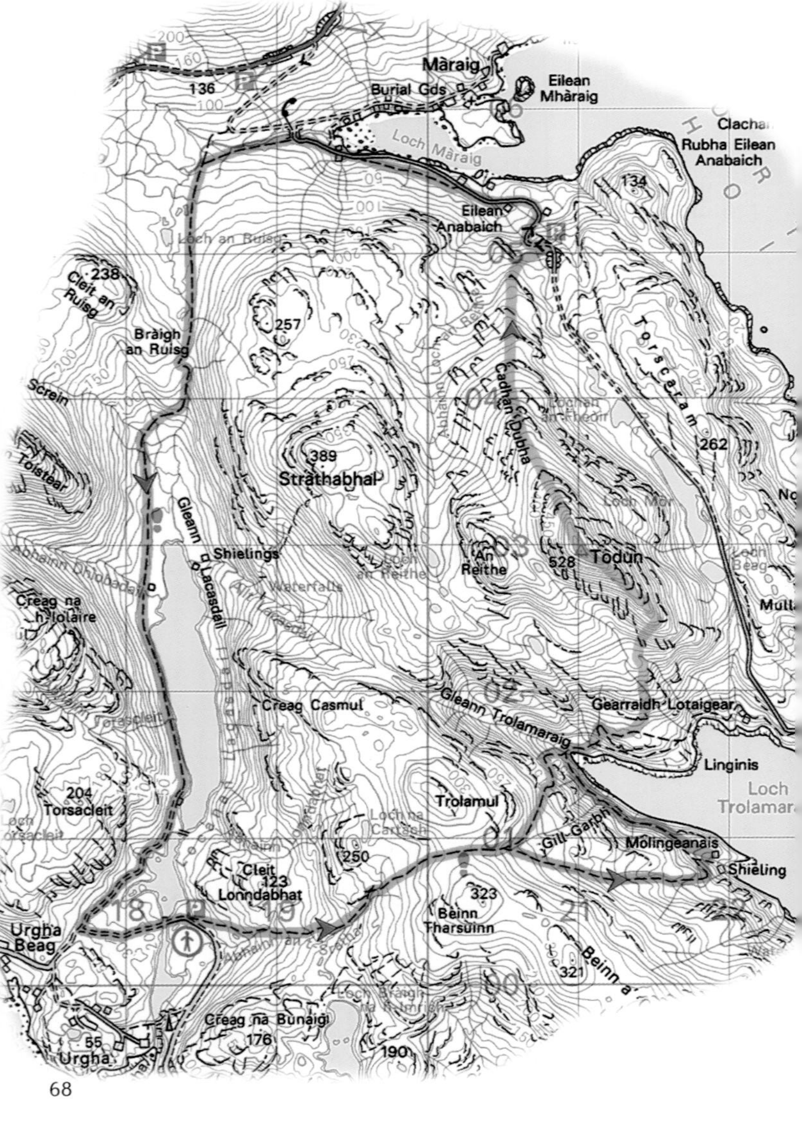
Màraig
Eilean Mhàraig
Burial Gds
136
Loch Màraig
Clachan
Rubha Eilean Anabaich
134
Eilean Anabaich
Loch an Ruisg
238
Cleit an Ruisg
Bràigh an Ruisg
257
Torscaram
Cadhan Dubha
Screin
Lochan an Fheòir
262
389
Strathabhal
Toistear
Loch Mòr
Gleann Lacasdail
Shielings
An Reithe
528
Todun
Loch an Reithe
Loch Beag
Waterfalls
Creag na h-Iolaire
Mulla
Creag Casmul
Gleann Trolamaraig
Gearraidh Lotaigear
Torascleit
Linginis
Loch Trolamara
204
Torsacleit
Loch Torsacleit
Trolamul
Loch na Cartach
Gill-Garbh
Mòlingeanais
250
Cleit
123
Lonndabhat
Shieling
323
Urgha Beag
Beinn Tharsuinn
321
Creag na Bùnaigi
176
55
Urgha
190

fence is required to keep the cattle in. Once you are ready to leave, locate a path that starts at a galvanised gate at the junction of fences at the northern end of the settlement. The path winds its way through steep ground above the sea, crossing **Gill Garbh** and another smaller stream which may be formidable obstacles after heavy rain. After a kilometre the path rejoins the main route just before the footbridge at the head of Loch Trolamaraig.

Tòdun from the southeast on the Reinigeadal path

A second footbridge that is unmarked even on the OS Explorer series crosses Abhainn Kerram and shortly afterwards a minor path drops away south towards the shore. Ignore this and continue on the higher track until you reach some barrel-shaped rocks. Leave the path here and head due north for the prominent ridge of Tòdun crossing the easy and often dry ravine of Allt Dubh. Slowly make your way up the steep southeast ridge of Tòdun, weaving in and out among the rocks and steep heather. ▶ The approach towards the summit of **Tòdun** narrows and then eases towards the trig point.

Take frequent breaks to enjoy the views east to the Shiant Islands and, on a clear day, to the Cuillin of Skye.

69

Cairn at the bealach in Bràigh an Ruisg

Descend NNW over the easier slopes of **Cadhan Dubha** using the compass to avoid being fooled by the sloping ground and led off too far to the west. Aim to come out onto the road near where it twists and turns and drops steeply down to run alongside **Loch Màraig**.

From sea level at the head of Loch Trolamaraig, an ascent of Tòdun may seem an awesome prospect. However, anyone wanting a less arduous walk can easily avoid it by continuing along the path around the head of Loch Trolamaraig until reaching the road and then following the road north towards Màraig.

Above Loch Màraig the road goes through a narrow cutting, giving a fine viewpoint north towards Eilean Shìophort. It is possible to follow the line of the road westward to the head of the loch using a short footpath that starts just beyond the stream at **Eilean Anabaich** and runs south of the road for 800m. Back on the road, carry on westwards until just before the bridge, and take the path back to Urgha which is signposted on a gate on the left. The path continues westwards through another gate for

600m then turns south through **Bràigh an Ruisg**. The surface is excellent throughout and further south this route would almost certainly be designated as a bridleway.

There is a cairn to mark the highest point on the route before a gentle descent passes the lochans of **Gleann Lacasdail** and reaches the road at **Urgha**. Turn left to return to the starting point.

Viewed from Molingeanais in late afternoon, the shadow cast by **Kerram** (NB209019) resembles the profile of a face with a prominent nose and is locally known as Sron an t-Siorraim – the Sheriff's Nose – although no one seems to know who he was.

THE GATLIFF TRUST

The independent hostel at Reinigeadal is well worth considering for those who want remote and budget-priced accommodation. It is part of the legacy of a remarkable, if uncompromising, man. Herbert Gatliff (1897–1977) was a soldier and then career civil servant with left-of-centre leanings who became heavily involved in various conservation and outdoor organisations such as the Ramblers Association, the National Trust and the Youth Hostels Association. In 1953 early retirement freed him from officialdom and he was able to pursue his passion for the countryside and access. Throughout the 50s and 60s he made frequent visits to the Hebrides each September, always ending on Iona. In 1961 he set up the Gatliff Trust to perpetuate his various interests, particularly those of providing youngsters with cheap hostel accommodation in remote areas. Realising the lack of hostels on the islands and endeavouring to use funds in ways of which Herbert would have approved, the Trustees set about establishing a string of hostels in the Outer Hebrides. Today there are four; Reinigeadal; Gearrannan on Lewis; Howmore on South Uist and Berneray. There have been others on Scarp off the west coast of Harris and Baleshare on North Uist, but these have since closed. However, there are plans to open more.

Today the hostels are run by the Gatliff Hebridean Hostels Trust working in close association with the Scottish Youth Hostels Association. No advanced bookings are accepted but although accommodation is limited, there is a policy to give everyone a welcome. Camping is also allowed. See www.gatliff.org.uk for further details.

WALK 8
Cleit Ard

Start/Finish	At the car parking and picnic spot at the side of the A859 (NB195065)
Highest point	Cleit Ard 328m/1075ft
Climb	190m/622ft
Distance	6km/4 miles
Time	1½–2hrs
Map	OS Explorer 456; OS Landranger 13 or 14
Refreshments	The hotels and tea rooms of Tarbert

Although a short route and an easy climb, the summit of Cleit Ard gives fine views north and south along Loch Seaforth. This 23km-long sea loch marks the boundary between Harris and south-east Lewis and is positively fjord-like, hence its name Loch Seaforth, or Loch Sìophort (*fjord* is old Norse for firth or forth). As an alternative, an ascent of Cleit Ard could start and finish from the north side, parking a vehicle alongside the road near the bridge over the Abhainn Scaladail (183098) and taking the path that leaves the road beneath Caisteal Ard at 186096. The approach from the south described here offers better off-road parking on sections of the old main road.

Rest awhile and take in the magnificent views: An Cliseam and its neighbours to the west, Tòdun to the south and Bheinn Mhòr prominent across Loch Seaforth.

Walk north up the road until the old road bears off left at the radio mast below **Gormul Màraig**. After 200m take the footpath that leads north-west to Lochan Cleit Ard. Continue along the path, passing a third unnamed lochan, then strike off right up the firmer ground of Cleit Ard's north-west ridge. The ground becomes rockier with height but is never difficult. The summit itself is marked by a cairn. ◄

If visibility is good it is possible to see the fertile, green pasture at **Ceann Mòr** (223067) on the opposite shore of Loch Seaforth trapped between Tòb a Tuath na Ceanna

Mhòire and Tòb a Deas na Ceannamhoire. Ceann Mòr was one of over 30 townships systematically cleared to make way for the Park sheep farm in the first half of the 19th century. With the aid of binoculars a further two less prominent townships can be picked out further north along the loch at Gil Mhic Phaic (217083) and Sgaladal Bheag (220100).

Cleit Ard from Loch Màraig

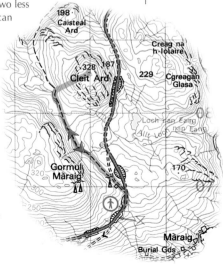

When you are ready to leave, drop down the north-west ridge, regain the path and head back south to the A859. Alternatively, pick your way down the south ridge to make the best of the views.

PRINCE CHARLES EDWARD STEWART AND LOCH SEAFORTH

After his supporters were decisively beaten at Culloden on 16 April 1746, the 25-year-old Bonnie Prince Charlie eluded capture and in the months that followed roamed across the Hebrides aided by various clansmen. Despite a price of £30,000 on his head, Charles kept one step ahead of the government troops that pursued him by land and sea. He rarely stayed in one place for long and followed an erratic course, sleeping in primitive shelters and caves known to his companions. On 30 April 1746 he arrived on Scalpay at the mouth of Loch Seaforth and was concealed there for three days while his supporters went up to Stornoway to secure a boat to escape to France.

After receiving a messenger with news that a boat had indeed been found, the Prince left Scalpay on 4th May accompanied by a handful of supporters and headed up Loch Seaforth, landing at the head of the loch. The only way to get to Stornoway was to walk. Unfortunately the guide lost his way, night came down and in the darkness they found themselves surrounded by bog and water. At last they reached a point some three miles from Stornoway where they took shelter by the side of a loch, known since as *Lochan a Phrionnsa*, 'The Prince's Loch'. By the time they arrived, the gentlemen of Stornoway were undecided about what to do – capture the Prince or provide a vessel – and they simply allowed him to escape in a rowing boat on 6th May.

Two months later, the most famous incident of the chase happened when Flora MacDonald of South Uist escorted him, disguised as her maid, across to the Isle of Skye closely pursued by the militia. At last, on September 19th, Prince Charles was picked up by a French ship near Arisaig on the mainland and he sailed away never to return to Scotland. He lived for another 42 years, moving around Europe in a range of guises. He had a daughter by his lover Clementina Walkinshaw in October 1753, but the relationship ended in 1760 amid tales of jealousy and violence. He married a 19-year-old German princess, Louise of Stolberg, in 1772 but it was to end without producing a child. He died in Rome in January 1788 after a largely dissolute, drunken life that many said was a direct result of the amount of whisky he consumed in the Highlands and Islands.

WALK 9
Liuthaid and Mullach a' Ruisg

Start/Finish	On the A859 near Abhainn Bhiogadail (NB187116)
Highest point	Mula Chlainn Neil 492m/1614ft
Climb	578m/1892ft
Distance	10 km/6 miles
Time	4hrs
Map	OS Explorer 456; OS Landranger 14
Refreshments	Various cafés and hotels in Tarbert and Aird Asaig

There are over 4000 freshwater lochs marked on the OS Explorer series of maps for Harris and Lewis. Loch Langabhat, 'long loch', is the largest with a length of 13km, covering an area of 8.9km². It offers good fishing for brown trout and salmon, which enter the loch from its northern end at Griomarstadh. Just like the loch, this walk straddles the border between Harris and Lewis and takes in the summits at its southern end that are not covered by other routes. These are Mula Chlainn Neil and Mullach Bhìogadail, which are the north and south summits of Liuthaid respectively, and Mullach a' Ruisg. Being outliers, the walk provides excellent views in all directions, and being well covered in grass, these hills are a good place to see wildlife. On a clear spring morning I sent up a number of golden plover, whose alarm calls suggested they may have been nesting, disturbed a mountain hare still showing signs of its white winter coat and saw a number of red deer on the slopes below the main ridge.

Walk along the main road to **Loidse Ath Linne**, then turn north-west up the track that leads to the shore of Loch Langabhat and follow it until just below the bealach level with ruined shielings at Airigh Lag a' Chrotha at 185136 (only shown on the Explorer map). Find a place where you can safely cross the streams that feed into **Abhainn a' Mhuil** and climb the steep slope that leads to the cairned summit of Mula Chlainn Neil, the northern summit of Liuthaid. It is

75

Liuthaid and Mullach a' Ruisg above Àird a' Mhulaidh

tough going, so rest awhile to savour the fine views along Loch Seaforth and use the promise of a similarly fine view along Loch Langabhat to keep you going. After all that hard work, reaching **Mullach Bhìogadail**, the southern summit of Liuthaid, is an easy stroll. From here, pick up the line of metal fence posts that runs south-west to the pile of stones that marks the

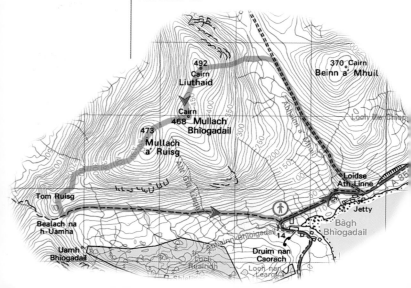

summit of **Mullach a' Ruisg**, 'the bare summit'. Continue south-west down the ridge to **Tom Ruisg** in Bealach na h-Uamha, 'the pass of the cave', the cave that gives the pass its name being Uamh Bhìogadail some 700m to the south. Pick up the stalker's path just to the south of Loch Ruisg and follow it eastwards back to the starting point.

GOLDEN EAGLE

The North Harris hills have almost the highest density of nesting golden eagles in Europe. While you can never be totally sure of seeing one, if you spend a few days here you will be unlucky not to see one. Soaring majestically on thermals with their wings outstretched to over 2m, they are a thrilling spectacle and you will never forget the first time you see one. Neither will you ever tire of seeing them thereafter.

Much of its diet is made up of medium-sized mammals and birds, most notably mountain hares and grouse, although in winter it may resort to carrion. But, contrary to some beliefs, the golden eagle rarely takes live lambs. During the 18th century it was intensely persecuted by gamekeepers intent on keeping grouse for the guns. Then in the second half of the 20th century their ingestion of sheep carrion contaminated with dieldrin sheep-dip reduced breeding success. But blanket afforestation that robbed them of their hunting grounds probably caused the greatest damage to the population. Without much in the way of trees, Harris has always been a stronghold for them.

An Cliseam from the summit of Liuthaid

WALK 10

The Skeaudale Horseshoe

Start/Finish	Scott Road, Tarbert, behind the Harris Hotel NB152002
Highest point	Sgaoth Aird 559m/1834ft
Climb	1022m/3300ft
Distance	15.5km/10 miles
Time	6½–7hrs
Map	OS Explorer 456; OS Landranger 14
Refreshments	Various cafés and hotels in Tarbert and Aird Asaig

The area bound by Gleann Lacasdail on the east, Loch a Siar to the west and the main A859 to the north contains two short strings of hills that can be linked by crossing Bealach Garbh to produce a horseshoe walk along pleasant ridges with fine views throughout. There is only one small problem: a direct ascent or descent to or from the summit of Gillaval Dubh to the bridge at Ceann an Ora involves an unpleasant scramble up very steep grass and through a band of rock. While still maintaining the integrity of walking a high-level horseshoe, the walk described here uses a gentler ascent directly from Tarbert. Even so, this route should not be underestimated. It may not be part of the main group of hills, but it still involves over a 1000m of ascent and will take up most of the day.

On a clear day, the views out to sea on both the east and west sides of Harris make all the energy expended in the climb from Tarbert worthwhile.

Cross the stile, pass over the footbridge and head for the gate behind the **mast** that leads on to the open hillside. There is a raised path that follows East Tarbert Burn but eventually this peters out and there is nothing for it but to strike out across the rock slabs and head for the skyline. At around the 350m contour the gradient eases and it is time to head north-west across the top of Cnoc Eadar Dà Bheinn to reach Gillaval Dubh, which is the first summit of the horseshoe. Head back south-east along the ridge to reach the summit of Giolabhal Glas, which is 100m north of the walled trig point. ◄

The ridge is broad and dry giving easy walking and after passing a couple of small lochans, you soon get to the foot of **Beinn na Teanga**. Either scramble up through the easy rock bands directly to the summit or make use of the easier grassy slope to the south. As you leave the summit, the whaleback hill of Tòdun faces you with the Shiant Islands out to sea. As you approach **Bealach Garbh**, avoid the easier ground on the left as it tends to force you down into Glen Skeaudale and you will only have to regain the lost height. If you look west over the northern tip of Taransay, on a clear day you may get a view of St Kilda. From this direction it looks more of a long whaleback of an island rather than the dramatic pinnacle typically seen in photographs, but it is the real thing with Boreray just to the north.

The ascent of **Sgaoth Aird**, 'high wing', is gentle. The walled cairn at its summit is lined with moss and resembles a bird's nest, providing shelter and relative warmth in poor weather. If it is a fine day you will be drawn to the edge of the summit plateau where there are good views down into Loch Seaforth, north to the peat land of Lewis and across to the Harris hills, which seem so close you could almost reach across and touch them. The descent to the west is rock-strewn but easy going and you soon arrive

Looking west from the summit of Giolabhal Glas with the summit of Uisgneabhal Mòr prominent on the right

at the bealach. The summit of An Cliseam is only 3km away and this is the ideal spot for a photograph, perhaps framing the small lochans that nestle in the bealach as foreground interest.

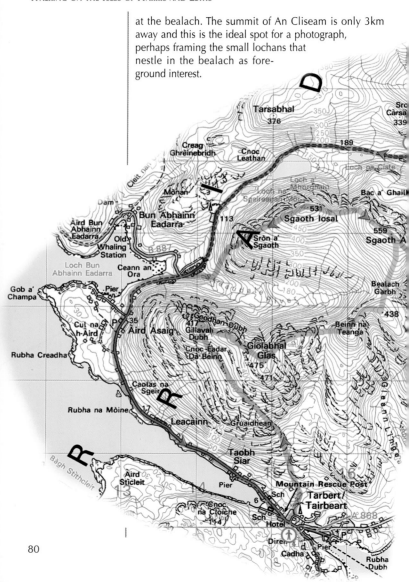

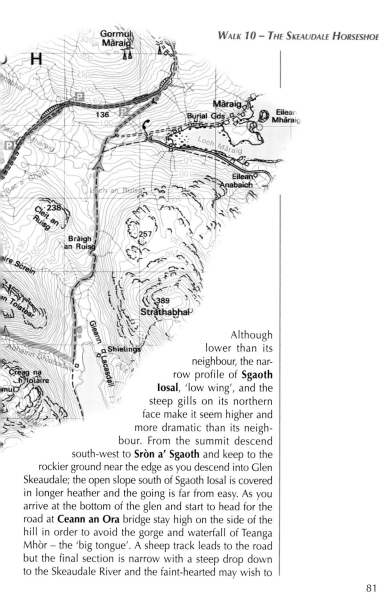

Although lower than its neighbour, the narrow profile of **Sgaoth Iosal**, 'low wing', and the steep gills on its northern face make it seem higher and more dramatic than its neighbour. From the summit descend south-west to **Sròn a' Sgaoth** and keep to the rockier ground near the edge as you descend into Glen Skeaudale; the open slope south of Sgaoth Iosal is covered in longer heather and the going is far from easy. As you arrive at the bottom of the glen and start to head for the road at **Ceann an Ora** bridge stay high on the side of the hill in order to avoid the gorge and waterfall of Teanga Mhòr – the 'big tongue'. A sheep track leads to the road but the final section is narrow with a steep drop down to the Skeaudale River and the faint-hearted may wish to

81

Giolabhal Glas from East Loch Tarbert

retreat to higher ground. Once on the road, turn left for Tarbert, perhaps stopping for ice-cream at the shop at Aird Asaig. The road walk passes remarkably swiftly, especially if you pass the time looking for birdlife. At the right time of year it is possible to see redwing, curlew, golden plover, lapwing, rock pipit, wheatear and even a golden eagle on the way back to Tarbert.

Alternative Route – The northern section of the Skeaudale Horseshoe from Màraig (16km/10 miles)

Park at one of the many parking places on the A859 between Loch na Ciste and the road junction for Màraig and walk south to **Ceann an Ora** bridge (NB138034) making use of the old road whenever possible. Climb up north-east to the summit of Sròn a' Sgaoth and reverse the previous route over Sgaoth Iosal and Sgaoth Aird until you can see into Glen Dhiobadail. The initial part of the descent below **Sròn an Toistear** is rocky and steep but as you approach **Abhainn Dhiobadail** the gradient eases and you soon reach the track alongside **Lochannan Lacasdail**. Turn north and climb over **Bràigh an Ruisg** before dropping down to join the road. A detour to the road end at Màraig makes a pleasant diversion with good views across Loch Seaforth to the rocky slopes of Caiteseal. Otherwise climb the hill to the main road and retrace your steps to where you started.

WALK 11

An Cliseam Horseshoe from Àird a' Mhulaidh

Start/Finish	On the A859 beneath Caisteal Ard (NB187096)
Highest point	An Cliseam 799m/2621ft
Climb	1065m/3450ft
Distance	13.5km/8½ miles
Time	6–7hrs
Map	OS Explorer 456; OS Landranger 14
Refreshments	Various cafés and hotels in Tarbert and Aird Asaig

Most people ascend An Cliseam by a direct assault from the south-east leaving their vehicle at one of the many good parking places along the A859. It is a short, sharp climb, gaining some 650m in 3km and fine if you have only a couple of hours to spare. As you near the summit, there is an unpleasant boulder field to negotiate and it is possible that ascending this direct route deters many visitors from considering hill walking in Harris ever again. There are better ways to climb An Cliseam.

This route makes a day of it, steadily gaining height at a more leisurely pace and arriving at An Cliseam from the north-west along the ridge formed by Mullach an Langa, Mulla bho Thuath and Mulla bho Dheas. There are a number of sections that involve some easy scrambling and others that are best avoided by dropping off the rock to gain a lower path. Anyone who is confident moving on rock will enjoy the route, but it is no place for novices, especially in poor visibility. But on a clear day, a traverse of the ridge with An Cliseam in front of you and the view of West Loch Tarbert, Taransay and the Atlantic Ocean unfolding below you is one that will be remembered for a long time. As a fellow walker once said, 'It's one for the connoisseur'.

Walk down the hill to the bridge and pick up the path that heads up **Gleann Sgaladail** along the north side of **Abhainn Sgaladail**. Don't be too concerned that the path is unmarked on the OS Landranger series and is shown as petering out on the OS Explorer series. It

Mulla bho Dheas, An t-Isean and An Cliseam from across Loch Bun Abhainn Eadarra

This is certainly the hardest section of the entire horseshoe, but as you work your way towards the top, the views to the north and east will make it all worthwhile.

exists and although it can be muddy after heavy rain it is easy to follow all the way up to **Loch Mhisteam**. At this point it does disappear and you are left to pick your way to the east ridge of **Mullach an Langa**. The ascent starts easily enough but soon encounters steeper grass and boulders near the summit. ◄ From the summit continue south along the ridge, passing over some boulders to gain the summit of **Mulla bho Thuath**. Descend southwards to the bealach, passing over a distinctive band of quartz, then follow the ridge as it turns southeast to the summit of **Mulla bho Dheas**. An exposed path leaves the northern side of the summit and heads east towards An Cliseam or you can navigate the crags along the eastern ridge and descend to the bealach below An t-Isean (146077), which is a prominent outcrop although it is unnamed on the OS Landranger map. From here it is a short ascent to the summit of **An Cliseam**, the last few hundred metres involving a scramble through jagged boulders.

Leave the summit by descending to the south-east until you are safely through the band of crags that probably give An Cliseam its name, which translates as 'rocky cliff'. Once onto easier ground, maintain height and traverse around the head of **Allt Tomnabhal**. Skirt below the prominent rock slabs on the south-eastern slopes of Tomnabhal, keeping to the easier ground before swinging around to the north-east to make for the two small lochans (184083) that lie directly to the west of **Cleit Ard**.

▶ From the lochans it is 1.5km northwards along the track back to the main road.

There is a bench here where you can rest your weary bones.

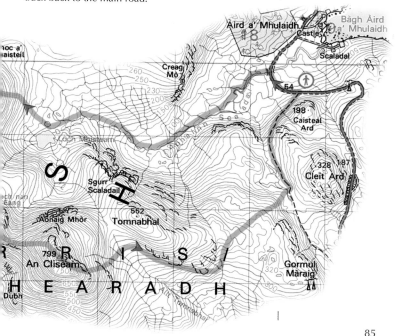

WALK 12
Stulabhal, Tèileasbhal and Uisgneabhal Mòr

Start/Finish	On the B887 near the bridge at the head of Loch Mhiabhaig (NB101062)
Highest point	Uisgneabhal Mòr 729m/2392ft
Climb	1400m/4585ft
Distance	21km/13 miles
Time	8hrs
Map	OS Explorer 456; OS Landranger 14
Refreshments	Various cafés and hotels in Tarbert and Aird Asaig

Gleann Chliostair, Gleann Mhiabhaig and Gleann Eadarra neatly divide the North Harris hills into four sections, each of which takes a full day to cover most of the major summits. The group to the east of Gleann Eadarra contains An Cliseam and was covered in the previous walk. Heading west, the next group lies between Glean Mhiabhaig and Gleann Eadarra and comprises three summits in excess of 600m that can easily be linked without losing too much height.

Stulabhal from the summit of Liuthaid

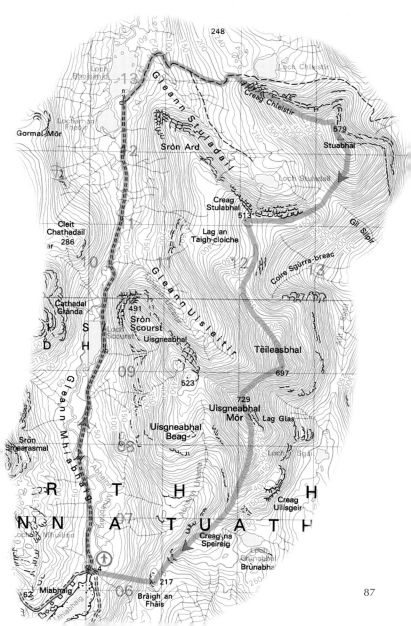

87

From the head of **Loch Mhiabhaig** follow the track north up **Gleann Mhiabhaig**, passing first below the impressive buttress of **Sron Scourst** and then the nose of **Sròn Ard**. This path is used by anglers to get to the inland lochs and is well maintained until it reaches the southern end of **Loch Bhoisimid**. Here, near the fishing hut, a smaller path snakes off to the north-east where it fords the **Stuladail** river before turning south-east directly towards Stulabhal. At the point the path starts to turn north-east towards Loch Chleistir leave it and ascend the north-west ridge of Creag Chleistir to the summit of **Stulabhal**. Initially the ground is steep and you will find yourself zig-zagging around rocky outcrops, but it soon eases to give a clear view of the summit which is marked by a trig point encircled by a stone wall, which can be a very welcome refuge on a windy day. ◀

There are good views to the north along Loch Langabhat.

Leave the summit on the south side and head down to the bealach between Loch Stuladail and Gil Slipir. Ascend the open slopes of the east ridge of **Creag Stulabhal** to reach its summit, then turn south around the head of Coire Sgùrra-breac and steadily climb the rock-strewn slopes to the summit of **Tèileasbhal**. After spending so long on the open hill side, the easy scrambling to reach the summit cairn comes as a welcome change.

From here the summit of **Uisgneabhal Mòr** is less than a kilometre away, albeit an energetic one, involving a sharp descent of 140m down to their shared bealach followed by a 180m climb over grass and boulders to the summit. ◀

The views westwards down into Gleann Uisleitir and eastwards across to An Cliseam and its neighbours give ample reason for frequent and much needed stops.

The final descent back to the road is less physically demanding, but needs careful navigation in mist. Leave the summit to the south, taking care to avoid the steeper slopes to the west and follow the broadening ridge as it sweeps down towards **Creag na Speireig**. The ground here can be very wet and it is best to go directly over the summit of Creag na Speireig and to keep to high ground as much as possible. Head north of Bràigh an Fhàis and pick your way through the rough ground to the south of **Abhainn Unasta** back to the start.

Uisgneabhal Mòr and Tèileasbhal from Beinn na Teanga

WALK 13

Muladal, Ulabhal, Oireabhal and Cleiseabhal

Start/Finish	Near the outflow of Lochan Beag on B887 (NB054077)
Highest point	Oireabhal 662m/2172ft
Climb	980m/3209ft
Distance	16km/10miles
Time	6hrs
Map	OS Explorer 456; OS Landranger 13 or 14
Refreshments	Various cafés and hotels in Tarbert and Aird Asaig, but nothing on the B887

Although slightly shorter and including fewer major summits, this route is very similar to Route 12 with a relatively easy outward leg using a good path up the glen followed by an excellent ridge walk. Both the ascent and descent are gentle, but once on the ridge there are excellent views and the option of an easy scramble to the top of the rock outcrop above Cathadail an Ear.

Approaching the summit of Ulabhal

Walk up the tarmac track that provides easy and rapid access to the dam at **Loch Chliostair**. From here the stalkers' path heads north, first along the eastern shore of Loch Chliostair and then the western shore of **Loch Aiseabhat**. This path gets you quickly and easily into the hills and up to a height of 240m with fine views northwards towards the Morsgail Forest. Without losing any height, leave the path at the head of Loch Aiseabhat and ascend directly to the summit of **Muladal**. Being one of the most northerly summits of the Harris hills,

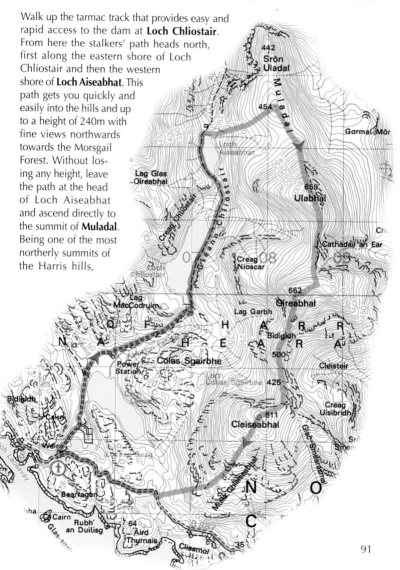

91

Looking down Cathadail an Ear to the snow-dusted summits of An Cliseam and its neighbours

this gently rounded hill provides good views across Lewis. For a more dramatic promontory, take a short detour 1km north to the summit of Sròn Uladal where there is steep ground on three sides.

From the summit of Muladal continue south and ascend the steeper north ridge of **Ulabhal** keeping to the easier ground on its north-eastern slopes to reach the mossy cairn that marks the summit. Descend the long southern ridge tracking slightly west above the dramatic **Cathadail an Ear** which has dramatic drops down into Gleann Mhiabhaig and a prominent rock outcrop that is an easy scramble, but can be avoided on the right. Climb south-west to the summit of **Oireabhal**. Again, leave the summit along the southern ridge tracking slightly west and ascend the rocky knoll of **Bìdigidh**. Repeat the procedure one more time, crossing the bealach marked on both series of OS maps with the spot height for 425m where there is the early sign of a path beginning to form. The next ascent involves a short, easy scramble through a rock band before swinging around to the west to gain the trig point at the summit of **Cleiseabhal**. ◀

Despite its modest height, the proximity of Cleiseabhal to the sea means it provides stunning views across to Taransay, all the way down the coast of South Harris and beyond to North Uist.

92

To avoid the steeper ground to the west, descend the long south-west ridge aiming for the island of Sòdhaigh Mòr. Once you reach **Mulla Chleiseabhal**, swing westwards to meet the road near **Loch nan Caor**. Walk along the road back to the start.

MOUNTAIN HARE

The mountain hare, described in the Introduction, is present in small numbers, so seeing one is a special treat. It is smaller than the brown hare, with a more rounded shape, and without a black upper surface on the tail. Mountain hares also have shorter ears and legs than the brown hare, and are mainly solitary, living high in the mountains, which is probably why they are a particular favourite with mountain walkers. We respect these hardy little creatures and their ability to survive severe weather, and take pleasure with every sighting, which is typically no more than a flash of blue disappearing over the mountainside.

They live in a 'form' (a depression in the ground), typically under the cover of heather or rock outcrops, but will burrow in snow and may congregate in larger groups for added warmth. In the breeding season between February and September, the female gives birth to a litter of up to five leverets after a gestation period of 50 days. The young are born with fur and their eyes open, and are weaned at three weeks.

WALK 14

Tiorga Mòr

Start/Finish	Near the outflow of Lochan Beag on B887 (NB054077)
Highest point	Tiorga Mòr 679m/2228ft
Climb	770m/2522ft
Distance	16km/10 miles
Time	6hrs
Map	OS Explorer 456; OS Landranger 13
Refreshments	Various cafés and hotels in Tarbert and Aird Asaig but nothing on the B887

In recent years there has been an annual Tiorga Mòr hill race that starts at the head of Loch Leòsaid, ascends the mountain by its steep southern flank then descends to Loch Aiseabhat and finishes at the dam. To get amongst the medals you would need to complete the route in less than an hour. This route is far more leisurely. It uses the path to get to the head of Gleann Leòsaid and then ascends the easier slopes to Bràigh Bheagarais and takes the excellent west ridge to the summit. The second part of the route gives good views of the overhanging buttress of Sròn Uladal before returning to the start on the stalker's path.

For those confident moving on rock, the southern slopes of Tiorga Mòr offer some low-grade scrambling and a direct route to the summit. Even if you encounter a section beyond your capabilities it is always possible to find a way around it on the steep grassy slopes.

Tiorga means a place where sheep were tarred prior to dipping.

Follow the tarmac track past **Lochan Beag** and to the footbridge over **Abhainn Leòsaid**. Leave the main track before the footbridge and follow the path up Gleann Leòsaid to the bealach. Although this path is clearly marked on the map, initially it is difficult to find anything resembling a path on the ground and you just have to head off in the general direction. Nearer the shielings (053095) it is much more distinct and provides easy walking up the bealach where there are good views down into Glen Cravadale and beyond to Scarp.

Leave the path and ascend the slopes between Sgarbh Choinneach and Abhainn Bràigh Bheagarais to reach **Loch Bràigh Bheagarais**. Keep to the higher ground around the loch and ascend to the highest point in Braigh Bheagarais from where there are distant views across Morsdail Forest and West Lewis. From here, pick your own way through the rocks to gain the north-west ridge of Tiorga Mòr. Initially the ascent is steep, but the angle soon eases and the final section, where the beginning of a path weaves between the rocks along the ridge, is a delight. ▶

The walled trig point at the summit of Tiorga Mòr provides shelter from the wind and a good refuge to enjoy the views that stretch out in every direction.

Tiorga Mòr from the main track

95

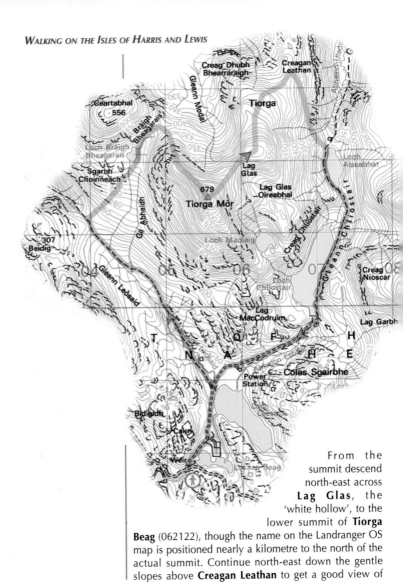

From the summit descend north-east across **Lag Glas**, the 'white hollow', to the lower summit of **Tiorga Beag** (062122), though the name on the Landranger OS map is positioned nearly a kilometre to the north of the actual summit. Continue north-east down the gentle slopes above **Creagan Leathan** to get a good view of

the daunting buttress of Sròn Uladal across the valley. Descend into Gleann Chliostair by turning south and navigating a route across the headwaters of **Abhainn Uladal** and the rock-strewn slopes to reach the stalker's path at the head of **Loch Aiseabhat**. Head south down the glen, passing the dam and the power station, to reach the road.

Looking south from Tiorga Mòr

WALK 15

*Huiseabhal Mòr, Oireabhal
and Huiseabhal Beag*

Start/Finish	Near the toilets at Huisinis (NA992121)
Highest point	Huiseabhal Mòr 489m/1604ft
Distance	14km/9 miles
Climb	825m/2700ft
Time	6hrs
Map	OS Explorer 456; OS Landranger 13
Refreshments	Various cafés and hotels in Tarbert and Aird Asaig but nothing on the B887

When it is washed by turquoise waves coming in from the Atlantic, many people would rank the silver beach of Tràigh Hùisinish as one of the most enchanting places anywhere in the world. The other beaches that can also be visited on this walk would also score fairly highly, so if it is a pleasant day you will undoubtedly want to wander along the shore and search among the rock pools. Because of this natural urge, the walk has been kept deliberately short, omitting Lèosabhal at the eastern end of the ridge, although it is easily incorporated if you feel like doing so.

The walk into and up Glen Cravadale is fairly flat so the ground can be covered quickly. You won't want to though; Crabhadail is a memorable place, and with those beaches to visit the first part of the walk may take some time. The ascent is gradual on a good terrain and the return leg along the top of the ridge gives fine views down onto nearby Scarp and, on a clear day, out to St Kilda, so you will definitely want to linger.

These toilets must be the most beautifully situated public conveniences in the UK – you could happily leave the door open to enjoy the view! Head north-east across the machair, famous for creeping willow and Scottish bluebells (harebells), and then pass through a gate to gain access

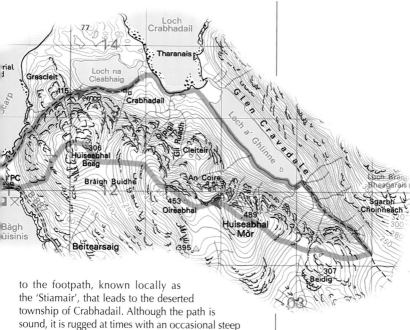

to the footpath, known locally as
the 'Stiamair', that leads to the deserted
township of Crabhadail. Although the path is
sound, it is rugged at times with an occasional steep
drop down to the sea, so move carefully and give plenty of
reassurance to the less confident in your party. At a junction in the path, strike out right up a pleasant little valley
towards **Loch na Cleabhaig**. Keep going past the cottage to
reach an unnamed beach which is backed by the old shielings and lazybeds of Crabhadail.

Leaving the coast, follow the indefinite path along
the southern shore of **Loch a' Ghlinne**, 'lake in the
glen', to reach some old shielings and a more definite
footpath at its southern end that climbs to the bealach,
criss-crossing Allt a' Ghlinne all the way up to the cairn.
Follow the path south-east until you reach a second
cairn on the flatter ground at the bealach (040111), then
turn west over the remains of an old wall and through
the rock slabs to the north of Beidig. The unnamed

Looking north from Oireabhal across Cleiteir

This hill is a little gem in that, although it is less than 500m high, the summit provides astounding views in all directions.

lochans are a favourite watering hole of red deer and if you move quietly and keep downwind of them, you may see some.

Continue up the grassy slopes to reach the summit of **Huiseabhal Mòr**. ◀ When you are ready to move off, keep heading west across the easy ground along the top of the crags to reach the summit of **Oireabhal**, where there appears to be indecision about where to build a cairn. There are the beginnings of one, but it appears to be on a lower point. Just below the summit on a fine May afternoon, we startled a golden eagle that was basking on the ground below a small step, and 50m later set up a mountain hare that was still shedding its winter coat. Keep heading west across the easy ground of **Bràigh Buidhe** to reach the cluster of lochans at the summit of **Huiseabhal Beag**, then descend the south-west slopes down to Huisinis.

LEWIS

Ruins of the chapel at Filiscleitir in North East Lewis (Walk 27)

INTRODUCTION

Uigen – a typical township in West Lewis

Lewis has neither Munros (Scottish mountains above 3000ft high) nor Corbetts (Scottish mountains between 2500 and 3000ft high that have a drop of at least 500ft on all sides). However, it does have Marilyns, the name given to British hills of any height with a drop of at least 150m on all sides. (The official list of Marilyns changes slightly from year to year, but there are considered to be approximately 1550 including the remote summits on St Kilda – and, yes, there is a growing list of persevering folk who have ticked them all off.)

The number of Marilyns in an area can be seen as a measure of the 'peakiness' or undulating nature of the land, as opposed to its altitude. If you want to be technical the word 'kurtosis' is used by statisticians to describe the peakiness of probability distributions. So we can say that although Lewis reaches no great height, it clearly has positive kurtosis as it boasts 27 Marilyns. In contrast, Harris, which most people would consider to be much more impressive, only has 17 Marilyns (unless you count the six on St Kilda, which is traditionally considered to belong to Harris). One of Harris's Marilyns is a Corbett and three are Grahams, (Scottish hills between 2000ft and 2500ft with a drop of 500ft on all sides), so rather than risk offending anyone, let's just call it a draw. A list of the Marilyns on Harris, Lewis and St Kilda is given in Appendix 4.

The hills around Uig in west Lewis have the highest density of Marilyns. It is a long drive to get to them down the B8011 from Gearraidh, which at nearly 50km is perhaps the longest cul-de-sac in the UK. But it is well worth it, offering a choice of routes and good views over the sands and out over the sea. Beinn Mhòr and its neighbours in the uninhabited Park area of south-east Lewis present more of a problem.

While it is easy to ascend Beinn Mhòr and nearby northern summits in a day from the road end at Eisgein (the final route in this book), getting to the remote southern hills in Park means either a long walk in and a multi-day camping expedition or hiring a boat from Tarbert to drop you off and collect you. It is essential to plan well ahead and be prepared to be ferried over at odd times of the day so that the boat operator can run his scheduled tourist trips. Who can question the logic of exchanging a few pounds for entry into one of Britain's last wildernesses? It has to be a good deal.

Many of the other walks in this section are unashamedly low-level and can be done in a few hours. They have been selected to take in the pre-history, such as Calanais and Dun Chàrlabhagh that every visitor comes to see, and to take you to the more remote corners of the island. But do not ignore the relics of everyday life that can be found all over Lewis.

Shielings on Lewis

In order to make the best use of the limited and typically poor quality land available, crofters used to take their livestock out to graze on the young heather and thin grasses that grow on the moorlands during the summer months, freeing up their more fertile lower land for crops to be grown and harvested. Some of the women accompanied the cattle and sheep, staying out on the moor in their shielings, while the men stayed behind to cultivate the crops, clean out the byres and make repairs to the main homestead.

Shielings are simply constructed dwellings about 12ft in length and 7ft wide. As building material is scarce on the moor, only the bottom half of the inner walls were made of stone, the outer and upper walls being made of turfs and sods of heather. The roof was also heather roots and turfs supported by a framework of whatever wood and timber was available. The fire was near the door but there were no windows. Furniture was scant; at best there was a wooden box for a table, piles of dry sods for seating and dry heather and grasses for a mattress.

The usual time to go to the shieling was mid-May, returning at the end of August when the cattle were taken into the enclosed winter grazing known as the 'fence'. The daily routine consisted of getting the fire going for breakfast, milking the cows and then taking the fresh milk back to the main house for the rest of the family.

Modern-day shieling at Cuidhsiadar (Walk 27)

The milk was covered with a sheep-skin with the wool removed from it, held across the top of the pail with string, called an 'imidal' to prevent it slopping over the pail. Imidals were always kept in salty water to keep them fresh and pliable.

Once home, a day's work had to be done on the croft, perhaps collecting seaweed to take back as a necessary salt supplement for the cattle. On returning to the shieling, the cows had to be herded and milked again before settling down for the night. They were a simple, but vital, part of the yearly cycle of subsistence agriculture.

The remaining walls of shielings can be seen all over the Lewis moorlands, many having been used until the 1930s and 1940s. In the Outer

Isles shielings were commonly known by their Gaelic name, airigh', and a cluster of shielings was a gearraidh. Even if their presence is not marked on the OS map by the all too obvious label of 'shielings', it is possible to work out where to find remains by looking for place names such as Airighean Thùlagabhal (NB315418) and Gearraidh a' Deas (NB473485) (marked on the OS Explorer map but not the Landranger) that just appear to float in the middle of seemingly empty OS grid squares. Confined indoors during inclement weather, 'shieling hunting' makes an enjoyable, if brief, diversion and allows you to derive some entertainment value from vast areas of map that you would probably not otherwise use. Enjoy!

WALK 16

Ceann Loch Rèasort from Loch Ròg Beag

Start/Finish	At the gate to Morsgail Lodge, about 1km from the B8011 (NB139238)
Highest point	130m/426ft
Climb	300m/982ft
Distance	18.5km/11½ miles
Time	5hrs
Map	OS Explorer 456 and 458; OS Landranger 13 or 14
Refreshments	The Calanais Visitor Centre is open Monday to Saturday from April to September but only from Wednesday to Saturday during the rest of the year.

Although this is a low-level walk, due to the poor terrain and occasional difficulties in crossing rivers, it is a serious undertaking and, without a GPS, navigation would be challenging in poor visibility. Unless it is freezing or has been exceptionally dry, even the paths marked on the OS maps are sodden and you will be exceptionally lucky not to have water come over the top of your boots. You have been warned!

But if you are not averse to some potentially challenging route-finding, crossing water courses and the odd wet sock, then this route has a lot to offer. Once away from the lodge, Morsgail Forest is a wilderness with few man-made things in view to break the spell. There are the beehive dwellings at Gearraidh Bheinn na Gile (132200) to visit en route and Ceann Loch Rèasort is an idyllic destination and an ideal spot for a leisurely lunch or an overnight camp. Loch Rèasort penetrates 9km inland and divides Harris and Lewis along their western boundary. *Ceann* is the Gaelic word for head, so it follows that Ceann Loch Rèasort is at the extreme end of the loch where there are a number of cottages, some of which were in use as remote holiday homes 30 years ago. Now they appear to have been purposefully made unusable with their doors and windows blocked up with stones. As this walk approaches Ceann Loch Rèasort from the north there are impressive views of the Harris hills on a clear day.

Recognising that most walkers will need to get back to their vehicle, the route also returns the same way. However, it is possible to reach Ceann Loch Reasort from the south using either of the main glens through the Harris hills to make a circular walk of nearly 30km. Alternatively you could pass through Ceann Loch Reasort as part of a traverse of West Lewis and North Harris.

Follow the main track down to Loidse Mhorsgail (Morsgail Lodge) for 1.5km as it snakes its way past the many weirs that have been built into this important salmon and trout river. Bear left over the bridge at the northern outflow of the loch to follow an indistinct path that runs along the eastern shore of **Loch Morsgail**. Follow the path around the loch to its south-west corner where another foot-bridge crosses **Abhainn a Lòin**. On meeting the path that runs down the western side of Loch Morsgail, turn south passing through a stone wall and past another weir to the remains of a footbridge that would, if it were there, take

Crossing the Abhainn Bheinn na Gile

you back to the eastern bank of Abhainn a Lòin. Cross the river as best you can and pick up the path on the other bank. There is a weir constructed from boulders held together with wire further upstream and this may be an option, but crossing Abhainn a Lòin can be difficult and dangerous when the river is high, and if you do not feel confident you should not attempt it. The route marked on the OS maps crosses the Abhainn a Lòin twice, first to the west bank and then back to the east bank so it is possible to walk this route without crossing it at all. To do this, leave Loch Morsgail at its south-east corner and traverse the rough ground below Sgalabhal Mula to regain the path just after the ruined footbridge.

From here keep following the path south, below the western slopes of **Scalabhal,** scattered with numerous tyres that have been put down at some time to improve traction for the all-terrain vehicles used to get around the estate. They are hideous and an intrusion into this wilderness, but there are few boulders and stones available that could be used to improve the drainage of the main paths, so it may have been an act of economic necessity or desperation.

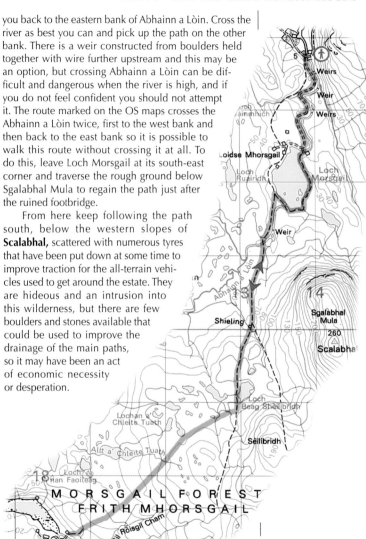

107

Soon after the ford at Gearraidh Bheinn na Gile (by a shieling marked on the Landranger map) there are remains of some beehive dwellings which are well worth exploring. Follow the right-hand fork in the path heading south-west to cross another ford through the outflow of **Loch Beag Shèlibridh**. Fords are a feature of this wet route and there are more to come! The path can be indistinct but keep heading south-west, negotiating the fords to the east of **Lochan a' Chleite Tuath** and through **Allt a' Chleite Tuath** before dropping down to **Loch Rèasort.**

Although it is occasionally way-marked with small cairns or marker posts, said to have been put there by the postman who took the mail to Ceann Loch Reasort, it is all too easy to lose the path as the view to the south is magnificent with a panorama of the mountains of North Harris running left to right: Stulabhal, Tèileasbhal, Sron Scourst and Oireabhal with the very prominent overhanging cliff of Sron Uladal.

After a leisurely lunch, it is back by the same route, negotiating the fords and sodden peat bog yet again. ◄

Callum an 'ic Asgaill from Luachair was awarded a British Empire Medal for walking to Morsgail three times a week to collect and deliver mail around the head of Loch Rèasort.

Emerging from a beehive dwelling at Gearraidh Bheinn na Gile

BEEHIVE DWELLINGS

Constructed very much like an igloo, but using rocks rather than ice, beehive dwellings can be found throughout the Hebrides, in Ireland and in other places across the world. They are all made using very similar methods, which date back to Neolithic times. Some are directly connected to others, presumably to give separate sleeping quarters or as a quick route to the neighbours, and most have a curved wall leading to the door in the windward side to keep out the worst of the weather. The lower layers of stone were laid horizontally while the upper courses were overlapped in decreasing concentric circles and finally capped with a copestone to give the beehive shape. Once covered in turves, they made an excellent windproof and waterproof shelter and, if you are happy to get a bit muddy, it is worth crawling into any of those still standing to experience what it must have been like living out on the moor.

Not all date back to other millennia; it is thought that many were constructed in the last few hundred years as summer shielings. With no wood available for roof supports, what else do you build for shelter except a stone igloo? For those who enjoy wilderness walking, there are particularly good examples at Both a Chlair Bhig, NB117148 and Both Ruadh, NB065217 with others scattered around the Aird Mhòr and Aird Bheag peninsulas north of Loch Rèasort.

WALK 17
Griomabhal, Naideabhal a-Muigh and Laibheal

Start/Finish	At the slipway at the road end, south of Mealasta (NA993234)
Highest point	Laibheal a Tuath 505m/1654ft
Climb	900m/2925ft
Distance	12km/7½ miles
Time	5hrs
Map	OS Explorer 458; OS Landranger 13
Refreshments	The Uig Community Shop at Timsgearraidh has a good selection of teas and coffees in its self-service machine and a toilet

This route covers the higher summits in the south-western quadrant of the Uig hills. The swirling contours and preponderance of outcrops marked on the map might suggest that walking on these hills is a trial rather than a pleasure. This is definitely not the case. For

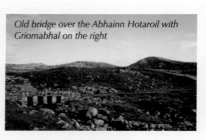

Old bridge over the Abhainn Hotaroil with Griomabhal on the right

the most part the terrain is rocky slabs, scattered boulders and short grass, so as long as you stick to the broader ridges and keep away from the steeper ground, walking here is very pleasant with the added bonus of views out to the Flannan Isles and St Kilda when visibility is good.

Although you are unlikely to meet many people in these hills today, the gleanns were once the main route between the townships on the coastal plain and the old settlements at Ceann Chuisil (NB038213), Tamanabhaigh (041203) and Aird Bheag (034196). The old path, which is occasionally marked by piles of stones, goes up Gleann Tealasdail, crosses Braighe Griomabhal and then descends into Gleann Tamanasdail and down to

Ceann Chuisil. Residents of the more remote settlements at Aird Bheag and Tamanabhaigh would usually continue their journeys from here by boat.

Alternatively, if people living around Loch Tamnabhaigh wanted to go to Stornoway, they walked eastwards to Ceannresort (NB107172), and then on to Morsgail to join the main road. The trip to Ceannreasort was undertaken three times a week by Iain Macdonald, the last resident crofter in Aird Bheag, to collect the mail. Anyone doing these walks today will appreciate the extraordinary fortitude of crofters who eked a living in such remote corners until relatively recent times, the last crofters leaving in the early 1950s. In recent years, the track over Bealach Raonasgail has brought people back to the area once again.

As the north face of Griomabhal, 'Grimm's fell', is steep and rocky it is best to follow the coast south from the slipway, crossing **Abhainn Ruadh**, Allt Foresgeo and Abhainn Stacageo, before starting the ascent of the west ridge of **Griomabhal**, passing over Tom an Eoin and loosely following a series of cairns to reach the walled trig point at the summit.

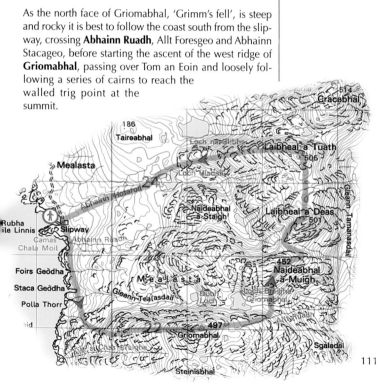

Loch Braighe Griomabhal with Naideabhal a Staigh and Mealaisbhal in the distance

As the crow flies, Naideabhal a-Muigh, the next summit, is just about 1km away, but getting there needs some care to avoid the steep slopes of Griomabhal. Descend the eastern ridge of Griomabhal to Gruaidh an Uillt Ruaidh (NB017221) and then follow the upper reaches of Allt Ruaidh until the gradient eases and you feel comfortable about heading due north across the flatter ground to the east of **Loch Braighe Griomabhal** before picking a route through the slabby rocks to the summit of **Naideabhal a-Muigh**.

The north face of Naideabhal a-Muigh above Gleann Ulladale Uachdrach is steep, so first descend to the north-east to reach a small lochan at the bealach and then ascend one of the two grassy runnels directly to the summit of **Laibheal a Deas**. The summit ridge between Laibheal a Deas and Laibheal a Tuath is peppered with lochans. Follow these to the northern summit of **Laibheal a Tuath** before descending westwards down the long west ridge to reach **Loch Uladail**. Pass the loch on its northern shore then cross the easy ground alongside the banks of **Abhainn Hotaroil** to reach the road.

This route can be combined with the following route to give a longer day in the hill covering 18km and taking the best part of 8hrs.

WALK 18

Mealaisbhal, Cracabhal and Laibheal a Tuath

Start/Finish	Near the ex-army blockhouse in the village of Breanais (NA993264)
Highest point	Mealaisbhal 574m/1883ft
Climb	1068m/3500ft
Distance	15km/9½ miles
Time	5–6hrs
Map	OS Explorer 458; OS Landranger 13
Refreshments	The Uig Community Shop at Timsgearraidh has a good selection of teas and coffees in its self-service machine, an excellent range of snacks in the shop and a toilet

If the Uig Hills are the hill-walking gems of Lewis, then Mealaisbhal, 'Farmstead fell', and Cracabhal, 'Crow fell', are the jewels in the crown. Although the highest peak in Lewis, Mealaisbhal itself is a fairly benign summit involving few difficulties other than a long ascent up easy slopes and band of large blocks of Lewisian gneiss at the summit. However, when combined with Cracabhal (514m), it becomes a different proposition with far more interesting terrain, and it makes a fairly challenging route if a direct ascent of the rocky northern slope of Cracabhal is included.

Leaving the road at the north end of **Breanais**, follow the peat track due east for 1.5km and then, keeping **Loch Sanndabhat** on your left climb to the saddle between **Mula Mac Sgiathain** and Mealaisbhal. Turn south and climb up to the summit of **Mealaisbhal**, which is marked by a cairn of large rocks. If you prefer not to scramble, keep to the easier ground on the left. ▶

Leave the summit and head down the south-east ridge of the mountain keeping to the easiest ground to the bealach and two lochans at Gualainn an Fhirich. These are not named on the OS Landranger series but are

On a clear day the views are unsurpassed, taking in the Harris hills to the south, the Flannan Isles and St Kilda to the west and Uig sands to the north.

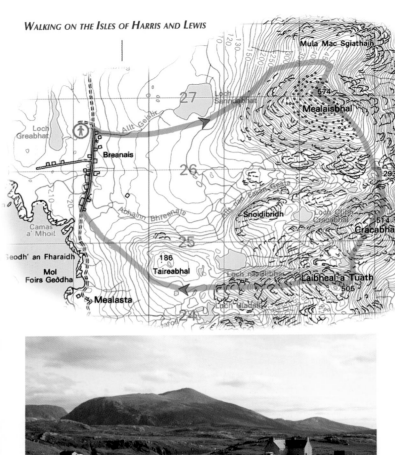

Mealaisbhal and Griomabhal from Mangurstadh

near to the spot height for 293m marked at NB032259. Ascending through the steeper rock on the northern slopes of Cracabhal looks more difficult than it actually is but if you are inexperienced in moving on steeper ground and lack confidence, it is best to head south-west from the bealach to skirt around **Loch Clibh Cracabhal**. From here there is a far easier ascent directly up the west ridge to the summit of **Cracabhal**.

Looking north to Mealaisbhal

Descend the southern ridge of Cracabhal passing a number of small lochans to reach a bigger lochan in the col at NB026247. Keep to the eastern shore of this lochan and climb up directly to the summit of **Laibheal a Tuath**. The long west ridge offers the easiest descent, striking out to gain an old path that passes south of **Tairebhal** and leads back to the road and Breanais.

ROUTES TO THE SUMMER SHIELINGS

The summer shielings and some earlier beehive dwellings used by villagers from Breanais and Islibhig can still be seen scattered around Cleite Fhìdigidh (NB061225). Some of the cattle and goods will have been ferried in and out by sea, landing at the head of Loch Tamnabhaigh, but the women and children made the annual trek on foot through the Uig hills. One of the main routes used started just south of Abhainn Bhreanais, skirted south of Tairebhal and Loch na Clibhe, passed between Cracabhal and Laibheal a Tuath to cross Bealach Raonasgail before taking a direct route down through Coire Diobadail to the shielings. Small cairns can still be found that mark this and other routes to the summer shielings.

Alternative low-level walk along the Gleann

There are lots of other walks in the area. Splitting the two chains of Uig Hills is the steep-sided valley of Gleann Reonasgail. A well-surfaced track runs the entire length of the valley starting on the road alongside a quarry at NB032312 and providing easy access right the way down to Loch Tamnabhaigh, where there is a relatively new house. Those who prefer low-level walking could make an entire day walking down this track and back, surrounded by dramatic scenery along the entire route. The round trip of some 21km only ever gets to 250m at its highest point and does this via the gentlest of ascents.

WALK 19
*Tamanasbhal, Teinneasabhal,
Tahabhal and Tarain*

Start/Finish	Near the cattle grid just past the distillery, south of Càrnais (NB033313)
Highest point	Tahabhal 515m/1690ft
Climb	1020m/3340ft
Distance	20km/12½ miles
Time	7hrs
Map	OS Explorer 458; OS Landranger 13
Refreshments	The Uig Community Shop at Timsgearraidh has a good selection of teas and coffees in its self-service machine. There is also a public toilet.

Compared with their neighbours across the valley, the Uig hills to the east of Gleann Reonasgail are seldom visited. Perhaps it is because they are slightly more landlocked and provide less opportunity for sweeping views down to sandy beaches and the Atlantic; possibly because it is a bit more of a walk in to reach them. If you only spend a short time in the district, then it is only natural to want to climb Mealaisbhal, which is a straightforward ascent from the coastal road to the west. But if you can spare more time, then a walk linking the 'three bhals' of Tamanasbhal, Teinneasabhal and Tahabhal with Tarain is extremely rewarding, providing a challenging day's walking with excellent views of both the local hills and the more distant Harris hills. Being remote, it is also a walk where there is a fair chance of seeing both eagles and red deer.

Follow the track south past **Loch Raonasgail** to the highest point on Bealach Raonasgail (035244). Look out for deer around Loch Brinneabhal on the way and, if it is at all windy, be prepared for strong gusts near the top of the bealach as the air is forced up the valley and through the

Heading up Gleann Reonasgail

narrow gap. Leave the track and ascend the north-west ridge of **Tamanasbhal** to its summit where there are dramatic views down to Loch Diobadail.

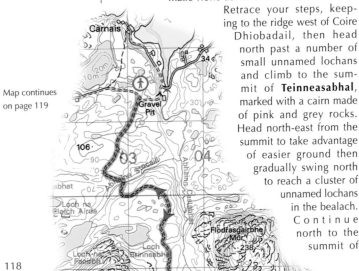

Map continues on page 119

Retrace your steps, keeping to the ridge west of Coire Dhiobadail, then head north past a number of small unnamed lochans and climb to the summit of **Teinneasabhal**, marked with a cairn made of pink and grey rocks. Head north-east from the summit to take advantage of easier ground then gradually swing north to reach a cluster of unnamed lochans in the bealach. Continue north to the summit of

Tahabhal
which, despite
being higher
than its neighbours,
has a less imposing cairn.
Again, depart from the summit heading north-east to take
advantage of easier ground and gradually swing north to
Loch Mòr Braigh an Tarain. ▶

   Continue north through slabby rocks to the summit of
Tarain and for the last time on this route, leave the summit
and head north-east towards Creag Stiogh an Fhais before
turning north to the unnamed lochans immediately south

This loch is said to
have pink water lilies
in flower in early
summer.

119

Tahabhal and Teinneasabhal

of **Cleite Adhamh**. Continuing north leads to difficult terrain beyond Flodrasgairbhe Mòr and would necessitate crossing the ever-widening Abhainn Caslabhat to return to the start point. It is easier to drop down to the west alongside **Allt Uamha Mhircil** and cross the Abhainn an Ath' Deirg while it is still relatively narrow and shallow in order to regain the track and return to the start.

LEWIS WHISKY

Although nowadays the sales of single malts are booming, you cannot buy a whisky from Lewis or Harris. However, this has not always been the case. In the early 1830s the Duke of Sutherland, Mr Stewart MacKenzie, and others established a distillery in Shoeburn Glen at a cost of £14,000. The indigenous population preferred whisky from smaller, illicit stills and ultimately the venture failed and the distillery buildings were converted into a stable block for Lews Castle, which was being built at the time.

Recently, a Lewis entrepreneur opened Red River distillery, named after its location beside Abhainn an Ath' Deirg at Càrnais. With local crofters to grow the barley and an ample supply of peaty water, there is everything needed to produce whisky and by 2020 it should be possible to enjoy a single malt from the Isle of Lewis.

WALK 20
Suaineabhal from Cairisiadar

Start/Finish	On the B8011 close to two small cottages to the north of Near Cairisiadar (NB095334)
Highest point	Suaineabhal 429m/1404ft
Climb	625m/2050ft
Distance	8.5km
Time	5hrs plus 2hrs for detour
Map	OS Explorer 458; OS Landranger 13
Refreshments	The Uig Community Shop at Timsgearraidh has a good selection of teas and coffees in its self-service machine and a toilet

Suaineabhal, 'Sweyn's fell', is a great rounded elephant of a mountain that dominates Tràigh Uuige (Uig Bay). The ascent is straightforward and it provides an ideal summit for anyone who just wants to gain height quickly and enjoy the view. However it is very exposed and it can be decidedly cold on the summit. So ensure you take windproof clothing even on a warm day. Rather than descend by the same way, this route makes a detour to the south and can include a visit to Bothan Mileabhat, a well-preserved beehive dwelling, before heading back to the start. Allow another two hours for this detour.

Go through the gate and follow the narrow peat road for a few hundred metres until it forks. Take the left-hand branch directly towards Suaineabhal. Head off south-west along the north bank of the Teurabrie river; turn south to Tom Dhomhnull (083316) and then ascend directly to the summit of **Suaineabhal**, keeping to the grass as much as possible. ▶ On a clear day there are glorious views across Uig Bay, out to the Flannan Isles and St Kilda and down to the mountains on the west side of Lewis and Harris with Loch Suaineabhal and Loch Gruineabhat prominent in the foreground. It is definitely worth the effort. If you need

The 300m climb seems to go on for ever until finally the summit cairn comes into view on the right.

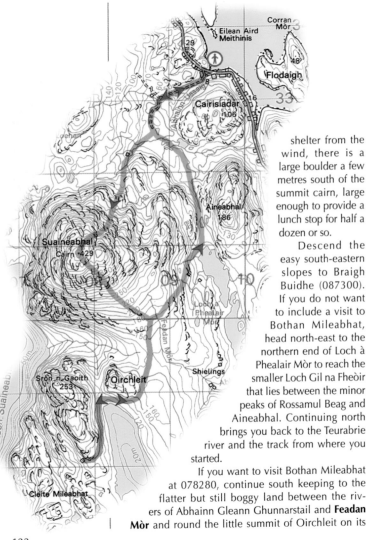

shelter from the wind, there is a large boulder a few metres south of the summit cairn, large enough to provide a lunch stop for half a dozen or so.

Descend the easy south-eastern slopes to Braigh Buidhe (087300). If you do not want to include a visit to Bothan Mileabhat, head north-east to the northern end of Loch à Phealair Mòr to reach the smaller Loch Gil na Fheòir that lies between the minor peaks of Rossamul Beag and Aineabhal. Continuing north brings you back to the Teurabrie river and the track from where you started.

If you want to visit Bothan Mileabhat at 078280, continue south keeping to the flatter but still boggy land between the rivers of Abhainn Gleann Ghunnarstail and **Feadan Mòr** and round the little summit of Oirchleit on its

eastern flank. Do not climb it, but follow the track at its base round the gravelly end of **Loch Gruineabhat**. From there veer right and away from the loch along a well-worn sheep track which is clearly visible. Keep to this path, following the marker stones which will lead you to Bothan Mileabhat, an intact *both* or beehive dwelling in the middle of a green, mossy patch.

Suaineabhal above Miabhaig jetty – a departure point for sea trips

To return, retrace your steps back as far as the head of Loch Gruineabhat following the marker stones. Always look out for the next one, it will be visible. They were originally placed there around 1920 by two ladies from Geisiadar to guide younger girls safely to the shielings. These stones lead across the dam that splits Loch à Phealair Mòr and eventually back to the road. But for a more direct route back to the start, retrace your steps to Braigh Buidhe and follow the return route described above.

Alternative ascent from Loch Suaineabhal

Park at the end of the road at NB063310, cross the dam and walk east for 500m passing south of Euscleit Mòr.

123

Summit of Suaineabhal looking down to Tràigh Uuige

Start to gain height by ascending north-east along the terrace marked as **Druim na Clibhe** (NB072315) on the OS Explorer series before gradually bearing right on to easier ground to gain the summit. Descend directly south into Gleann Ghunnarstail (NB075295) before turning north along the edge of Loch Suaineabhal following a sheep track. This route does involve some scrambling with steep drops down to the loch. As you approach the dam there are ruins of a group of beehive dwellings.

WALK 21
Bhalasaigh to Bostadh on Great Bernera

Start/Finish	To make this a circular walk it is best to start and finish in Breacleit where vehicles can be parked at the Community Centre and Museum (NB157367)
Highest point	Beinn an Tòib 60m/197ft
Climb	273m/894ft
Distance	11km/7 miles
Time	3hrs
Map	OS Explorer 458; OS Landranger 13
Refreshments	Available at the Museum but check opening times first (tel. 01851 612446)

Until the 150m wide Sruth Iasiadar was spanned by a bridge, the 400 or so residents of Great Bernera were effectively cut off from Lewis. Cattle had to swim across the straight to the mainland, and few Lewis folk bothered to venture there. The population lobbied for a causeway and even threatened to dynamite the cliffs on either side of the straight to provide the necessary rock. Fortunately this was avoided as funds were eventually made available to build the bridge, which was formally opened before a crowd of many thousands on Wednesday 22nd July 1953. This modest construction was a major innovation for civil engineering, being the first example in the UK of a bridge made of pre-stressed concrete girders. However, that does not seem to have been the main attraction; most people just wanted to promenade across and visit the other side.

In recent years Great Bernera has been owned by one of Scotland's most dashing and much loved aristocrats, Count Robin de la Lanne Mirrlees who, despite having other homes, prefers to live in a croft house on the island. After an action-packed life with romps through both military service and reputedly through the beds of willing socialites, he became the inspiration for Ian Fleming's James Bond. Mirrlees claims the title Prince of Incoronata, an area which includes a group of islands off the Dalmatian coast of the former Yugoslavia, which was given to him by the country's late King Peter II in the 1960s.

This circular route covers what is undoubtedly the best part of his Scottish kingdom. It may be small, measuring only six miles from north to south by about three miles from east to west, but on a calm summer day when the sparkling sandy beaches are washed by Caribbean-like turquoise waves, you could believe you were in the land of 007.

Leave the Community Centre and head off west along the road towards Tacleit, crossing the cattle grid and zig-zagging along the top of **Loch Barabhat** until the turn for Bhalasaigh is reached on the right. Continue through the small township of **Bhalasaigh** to the road end, then cross the footbridge that spans **Tòb Bhalasaigh**.

Turn right at the first house, passing through three gates. Follow the way markers north alongside Loch Veiravat, looking left along the shore of Camas Sanndaig at low tide to see remains of a stone lobster pond. Once you reach the road follow it north to **Tobson**, thought to be the oldest township on Great Bernera, then turn left for 150m before picking up the way markers as they lead you gently up the biggest ascent of the route at **Beinn an Tòib**. ◀ Continuing on past Carnan Gibegeo and through a gate in a stone wall, the path eventually drops into a small valley and follows the stream that flows north out of **Loch a Sgail**, 'the loch of the squall', to the deserted village of **Bostadh**.

The view west to the islands of Pabaigh Mòr and Bhacasaigh with the sweeping sands of Tràigh na Beirigh behind them is spectacular.

The stream is home to the dipper, a short stumpy bird that has the remarkable ability to enter fast-flowing streams and walk underwater in search of food.

Rest awhile, make use of the public conveniences if you need them and then wind your way back along the road to the start at Breacleit. At the turn for Tobson there is a cairn which was erected in 1992 to commemorate the Bernera riot of 1874, when a group of crofters stood up for their rights. In 1872 landowners reduced the amount of land available for summer grazing on mainland Lewis.

GREAT BERNERA/
BEARNARAIGH

THE DESERTED VILLAGE OF BOSTADH

But your attention will be drawn to the thatched structure at the back of the beach. In 1993 a severe storm cut away the dunes to leave a series of stone structures projecting through the sand. The archaeological department of the University of Edinburgh excavated the site in 1996 and found evidence of a Norse settlement. But underneath the Norse levels was a series of five Pictish 'jelly baby' or 'figure of eight' houses that were remarkably well preserved despite dating back to the second half of the first millennium – up to 1500 years old. What you see today is a reconstruction in a spot free of archaeological remains; the excavated houses have been reburied for preservation. Like the originals, its floor is well below ground level with the entrance at the southern end to keep out as much wind as possible. If you sneak a look inside you will see how they get their name. The basic style of construction does not differ significantly from that found in blackhouses built at the end of the 1800s, such as those on view at the Blackhouse Museum at Arnol and at Gearrannan. Some of the headstones in the cemetery above the beach tell tragic tales of lives lost at sea and early deaths from childbirth and diseases that science has now tamed.

Iron Age house at Bostadh

This was something that Bernera Crofters had enjoyed for centuries and although they put up and shut up first time around, further reductions 18 months later provoked an uprising, which became known as the 'Bernera Riot'. You can find out more, and enjoy some refreshments, at the Bernera Museum in Breacleit, which contains a verbatim account of the trial of three of the key Bernera men.

Looking north-west across Camas Bostadh

A LOCH OR A *TÒB?*

As you cross the bridge that spans Tòb Bhalasaigh, you will possibly be wondering why this stretch of water is not called a loch. The word *tòb* (pronounced 'tawp') is common throughout Lewis and Harris and comes from the Nordic word *hop* meaning 'tidal bay'. When the tide is turning and water is streaming under the bridge you can certainly see how Tòb Bhalasaigh gained its name. An-T-Ob, the stretch of water that provided the original name for what today is called Leverburgh down on the south coast of Harris, is another example of a tòb.

In the 19th century, lobster fishermen needed to store their catches ready to transport them to the lucrative markets to the south when the best prices could be found. They did this by building a tòb – a secure pond that was washed by the tide. The best local example is Tòb Blar Meadha, (NB173373), better known as the Great Bernera Lobster Pond. It is not named on either series of OS map although the dam is marked. The tòb was built in the 1860s by Murdo Morrison, a local man who ventured to Australia to earn enough money to employ a stonemason to build the dam. It is unique both for its size and the fact that it was used for at least 100 years until the arrival of refrigerated transportation. History lesson over – what you see before you at Bhalasaigh is a tòb, not a loch.

129

WALK 22

Calanais Standing Stones

Start/Finish	The car park at the Calanais Visitor Centre (NB213327), or either of the smaller car parks at Calanais II or Calanais III
Highest point	50m/164ft
Climb	Negligible
Distance	4k/2½ miles
Time	2hrs to give ample time to wander and reflect on exactly what happened here
Map	OS Explorer 458; OS Landranger 8 or 13
Refreshments	At the Visitor Centre which is open Monday to Saturday from April to September and from Wednesday to Saturday during the rest of the year

Few people are going to come to Lewis and not visit the Calanais Standing Stones. They are the icon of prehistory in the Western Isles. But what many people fail to appreciate is that there are actually two other satellite sites at Calanais. This short walk links all three sites and makes a good half-day out of what otherwise might have been a fleeting visit. Being low-level and never far from shelter or refreshments, it is also a choice for unsettled weather.

From the main visitor centre head east back towards the A858. Turn right at the junction following signs for Stornoway. After 200m take a minor road to the right before the road rises up towards Calanais III. This road is not sign-posted but there is a large boulder on the corner. After 500m the road ends. Walk through the gate and take a footpath 100m across a field. A second gate gives access to **Calanais II**, (Cnoc Ceann a' Ghàrraidh), marked on the OS

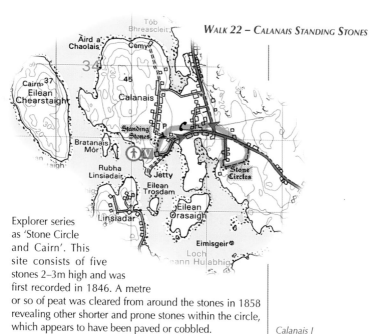

Explorer series as 'Stone Circle and Cairn'. This site consists of five stones 2–3m high and was first recorded in 1846. A metre or so of peat was cleared from around the stones in 1858 revealing other shorter and prone stones within the circle, which appears to have been paved or cobbled.

Calanais I

A well worn path leads 300m north-east to **Calanais III**, (Cnoc Fhillibhir Bheag), marked on the OS Explorer series as 'Stone Circle'. It has eight stones standing on its perimeter and four inside it. Being easily accessible from the main road, this site is said to attract more than its fair share of the mystically-minded who may find the main site too crowded with tourists on summer days. This has led to it being prominently featured in the writings of dowsers, earth energy enthusiasts and the like. The rock band Ultravox, led by Glaswegian Midge Ure, filmed part of a pop video here on a stormy day in January 1984 and used an equally dramatic image of the stones on the cover of their album, *Lament*.

To return to the main site and the visitor centre, simply cross the stile and turn left along the road. Climb the steep lane to the main stones and follow the perimeter path. This, the most famous site, contains around 50 stones in a cross-shaped setting. The impressive inner circle comprises 13 stones, the tallest of which is 4m high, and a small chambered cairn.

CALANAIS STONE CIRCLES

Without any sure knowledge, there are numerous theories about the meaning and purpose of stone circles such as those found at Calanais. Many people believe they were used in rituals relating to the moon, stars and the position of the distant hills. Whatever inspired their construction, all agree that the experience of visiting the Standing Stones of Calanais is not to be missed, especially during sunrise, sunset and at times when the moon is full. There are other sites in the Calanais group although nothing as complete as the main three. They are listed below. Given the preponderance of sites, perhaps it was just a case of keeping up with the neighbours – whatever they might be doing!

Calanais I – Stone Circle (NB211330)
Calanais II – Stone Circle (NB222326)
Calanais III – Stone Circle (NB225327)
Calanais IV – Stone Circle (NB230304)
Calanais V – Stone Row (NB234299)

Calanais II with the Harris hills on the horizon

Calanais VI – Stone Circle (NB247303)
Calanais VII – Ancient Village or Settlement (NB232302)
Calanais VIII – Standing Stone (NB164342)
Calanais IX – Standing Stones (NB233297)
Calanais X – Stone Circle (NB230336)
Calanais XI – Standing Stone (NB222356)
Calanais XII – Standing Stone (NB215350)
Calanais XIII – Stone Circle (NB215341)
Calanais XIV – Standing Stones (NB228329)
Calanais XV – Standing Stone (NB177346)
Calanais XVI – Standing Stone (NB213338)
Calanais XVII – Stone Circle (NB237320)
Calanais XIX – Stone Circle (NB218331)

WALK 23

*Dun Chàrlabhaigh and
the Gearrannan Blackhouses*

Start/Finish	To avoid the limited car parking at the visitor centres at Dun Chàrlabhaigh or Na Gearrannan, park near or at the Doune Braes Hotel (NB196401), but ask for permission if you intend to leave your car there all day
Highest point	70m/230ft
Climb	488m/1600ft
Distance	18km/11 miles
Time	5–6hrs giving plenty of time for sightseeing
Map	OS Explorer 459; OS Landranger 8
Refreshments	The Doune Braes Hotel and The Inn Between at Siabost are open all year including Sundays, but the café at Gearrannan is only open from May to September. There are no refreshments at the visitor centre at the Broch although there are toilets

Both Dun Chàrlabhaigh and the Gearrannan Blackhouses have stories to tell, but unless you happen to be a history buff, they are unlikely to hold your interest for more than half an hour at a time. Linking these two 'tourist attractions' on a circular route makes an enjoyable day out of what otherwise could easily be fleeting visits. The walk is also low-level and has ample opportunities for breaks for coffee and lunch, so it makes a suitable choice for a day when inclement weather deters all but the hardiest walkers from venturing in the hills. You can also split the walk in two, walking the northern loop as part of a visit to the blackhouses and the southern loop as part of a visit to the broch.

From the Doune Braes Hotel walk north towards Càrlabhagh to a path just after the last house on the right that heads off north-eastwards towards **Loch Fasgro**. Near the loch another path merges from the left. Ignore this and continue north passing left below a cairn until the road is reached. Once in Càrlabhagh,

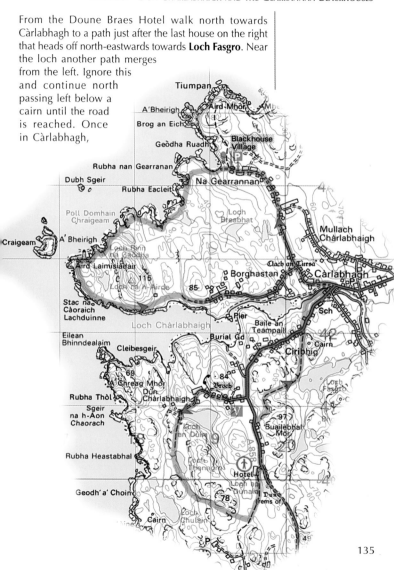

Tiumpan

A'Bheirigh · Aird Mhòr · Mh
Brog an Eich
Geòdha Ruadh · Blackhouse Village
Rubha nan Gearranan
Dubh Sgeir
Rubha Eacleit · Na Gearrannan
Poll Domhain Chraigeam
Craigeam · A' Bheirigh
Loch Raonn na Gedna
Aird Laimisiadair · 115
Loch na h-Airde · 85 · Borghastan · Clach an Tursa · Càrlabhagh
Stac na Càoraich Lachduinne · Loch Chàrlabhaigh · Pier · Baile an Teampaill · Sch
Eilean Bhinndealaim · Cleibesgeir · Burial Gd · Ciribhig · Cairn
69 · A' Chreag Mhòr · 84 · Broch
Rubha Thòl · Dùn Chàrlabhaigh
Sgeir na h-Aon Chaorach · Loch an Dùin · 97 · Buailebhal Mòr
Rubha Heastabhal · Coirc Thanagro · 78 · Hotel · Loch ba Dhunain · Dùn (rems of)
Geodh'a' Choin · Cairn · Loch Chulan

Loch Breabhat
Mullach Chàrlabhaigh
Loch Fasgro
A 858

135

turn left following signs to **Na Gearrannan** and continue to the road end and the **Blackhouse Village**.

When you are ready to depart, walk down towards the sea and head left through a gate and along the cliffs to the lighthouse at **Aird Laimisiadair**. The higher ground gives views to the west over Loch Ròg an Ear (East Loch Roag) to the islands of Craigeam, Campaigh, An t-Seana Bheinn and Beireasaigh and further south to the island of Bearnaraigh Beag (Little Bernera) with its beautiful white sands. ◀ Keep to the coast around the south side of **Loch na h-Airde** and Ben Laimisiadair past the township of Laimisiadair, one of the first to be cleared in Lewis in 1796. Eventually you reach a path below Ben Borrowston that leads through the crofts at **Borghastan.** Turn right at the T-junction and head towards Càrlabhagh and its two bridges; the left-hand one was built by Lord Leverhulme for a railway that was intended to carry fish from the once busy port of Càrlabhagh to Stornoway. Needless to say, the railway was never built but the intended route is now Pentland Road, possibly the most monotonous road in

On a clear day the Flannan Isles may be visible 30km away on the south-west horizon, where three lighthouse keepers famously disappeared in 1900 leaving a meal unfinished.

Dun Chàrlabhaigh

the UK. Turn right at the main road and head south to Dun Chàrlabhaigh. ▸

Head down through the crofts to the road end at **Loch an Dùin** where there is a little slab-and-pillar bridge that still does its job beautifully many generations after it was constructed. Take the left-hand gate and follow the track that leads south to the north-east corner of **Loch Thonagro**. A series of carefully placed flat stones to aid walkers over the wetter ground suggests that this was once a well-used route, probably frequented by children on their way to school. At the head of the loch the path peters out and turns into little more than a sheep track. At the gate keep to the left of the fence. Within a few metres there is a small stream which is easily crossed in a single stride with the help of two small, carefully placed boulders – further evidence that this was once a well-used route. Continue south around the loch, again keeping on the left side of the fence at a second gate, to pick up an indistinct stream that leads directly uphill to **Loch a Charnain Mhòr** (192397). Once past this little loch, which is shown but not named on the OS Landranger series, there is a better defined path that crosses the ground to the south-east. ▸ After a few hundred metres the track meets a much more defined gravelled roadway. At the junction turn left, heading north-east until The Doune Braes Hotel comes into view at the head of Loch an Dùnain.

Looking around the broch will provide ample time to recover for the last leg of the route.

There are good views across the open moor towards the township of Tolastadh a Chaolais which is dominated by the little outcrop of Beannan Mòr.

DUN CHÀRLABHAIGH – CARLOWAY BROCH

Evidence suggests that Dun Chàrlabhaigh was probably built some time in the last century BC. Two thousand years later, and much the worse for being stormed by raiders and pillaged for building materials, it still looks an imposing structure and a visible statement of status and power. It is thought to have been a defensible refuge that could house an extended family and their animals if they came under threat, much like a modern day air-raid shelter. It is not known how long it remained in use or when it fell into disrepair. It seems to have been still largely complete in the 1500s when some of the Morrison clan used it as a refuge from the MacAulay clan from whom they had been stealing cattle. The story goes that Donald Cam MacAulay climbed the broch by inserting dirks into the exterior wall and threw in burning heather, suffocating the Morrisons. The broch is next mentioned in a report by the local Minister in 1797. Dun Carloway featured prominently in reports on Western Isles brochs in the latter part of the 19th century and as a result it was one of the very first ancient monuments in Scotland to be taken into state care. But by then a large amount of material had been removed, probably for building blackhouses such as the one whose walls still stand below the access path.

From the car park the broch looks more or less like it would when it was built, albeit without a roof. The removal of material on the north side gives a cut-away section through the structure showing how it was made and what it would have been like to live there. The ground floor would have been for animals, with people living on the upper floors accessed by the stairs that spiral between the two thicknesses of wall. A conical roof of thatch or turfs on top of a double layer of well-crafted stonework would have made it a draught-proof and cosy refuge – well at least until a certain Mr MacAulay came asking about his lost cows.

GEARRANNAN BLACKHOUSES

Don't be fooled into thinking that what you see inside the Gearrannan blackhouses today is how it was when people lived there. Today they have plumbing and electricity and have been fitted out to such a comfortable standard that the Gearrannan Trust that runs them has little difficulty letting them as holiday homes. The hostel, run by the Gatliff Hebridean Hostels Trust in close association with the Scottish Youth Hostels Association, has a reputation of being one of the warmer hostels in the UK as it is heated by a ground-source heat-pump making it particularly attractive during the winter.

The last residents did not have such comforts and were happy to leave and move into the council houses up the road in 1974. Once vacated, the houses fell into disrepair until Urras nan Gearrannan (the Garenin Trust) was formed in 1989 in order to restore the village and to breathe life back into what was once a vibrant community. Traditional methods have been used to recreate the dry-stone masonry and thatched roofing of the original croft houses with the discrete integration of modern conveniences.

Gearrannan Blackhouses

The term *tigh dubh,* meaning blackhouse, only dates back to the middle of the 19th century. Prior to this time walls were of double thickness, built of stone and turf with thatched roofs. In the latter half of the 19th century a different design came into use with a single thickness of wall cemented with lime mortar. These were called *tigh geal,* meaning white house, and the antonym *tigh dubh* was then applied to the older houses in Lewis. They may look primitive but these houses have a number of clever design features. All the corners in the outside walls are rounded to soften the effect of the wind and the thatched roof does not overhang, leaving a distinctive ledge at the top of the wall called a *tobhta.* That way there is less chance of the wind getting under the thatch and ripping it off. It also gives a convenient platform for repairing or replacing the thatch, something that has to be done every couple of years. Great care was also taken to ensure that the walls leaned slightly outwards so that rain didn't penetrate into the interior. Given the materials available and the exposure to the Atlantic gales, it is inspired architecture.

WALK 24
West Side Coastal Path

Start	Na Gearrannan blackhouse village (NB192442)
Finish	Bragar School (NB295477)
Highest point	Aird Mhor 87m/285ft
Climb	536m/1755ft
Distance	18km/10 miles
Time	6hrs
Map	OS Explorer 460; OS Landranger 8
Refreshments	The Inn Between at Siabost and the Doune Braes Hotel just south of Càrlabhagh are open all year including Sundays. Otherwise opportunities for food and drink are few and far between on the west side of Lewis. The café at Gearrannan is open Mondays to Saturdays from May to September and the Morven Gallery just north of Barabhas is open Mondays to Saturdays from April through to the end of September

This waymarked route crosses some stunning beaches as it winds its way between the townships on the west side of Lewis, making best use of old pathways wherever possible. It is never far from a road end, so it can be easily cut short in poor weather, or split into shorter walks which can be easily fitted into a day of sightseeing. The West Side Circular bus route passes along the main road in both directions with frequent services around school times so you can easily get back to the start. Better still, park up first and take the bus to the start removing any doubt about missing a bus later in the day. Check the current timetables online at www.cne-siar.gov.uk/travel/ or pick up a copy at a local tourist information office.

See the previous walk for information about the blackhouses.

Walk down through **Gearrannan** village to the information board, go through the gate and follow the marker posts over **Aird Mhòr** and **Aird Mheadhonach**. This first section can be very wet underfoot and fording Fivig Burn and Allt na Muilne can require a diversion inland to find a suitable crossing place. Beside the views out to sea, there are a couple of interesting features to look out for. The first is the remains of an illicit whisky still, concealed behind some boulders on Aird Mhòr (194453). Locating this will test your navigation skills or require a GPS, but you cannot help noticing the pinnacle-like stack of Stac a Chasteil (202454) joined to the cliffs by a rocky arête. Sometime between 200BC and 200AD a blackhouse was built on the stack and there is evidence of defensive walls separating it from the mainland.

The path eventually traverses around Beinn Bheag and follows a descending route around the back to Bagh Dhail Mor to reach the road. Don't be too surprised if this section takes a disproportionate amount of time; the terrain improves from here.

Descending to Bàgh Dhail Mòr

141

Walk up the road to an information board and follow the marker posts up over the better ground between Cnoc na Moine and Creag an Taghain. As you approach **Dail Beag** the route turns inland alongside a fence to a stile and down to a footbridge that spans **Allt Dhail Beag**. Walk down towards the beach to pick up the marker posts at the picnic site and follow them directly up the open hillside to a stile and across the easy ground of Tom Tolalge, Carnagil Bhàn and Druim Bratag. The cliffs are dramatic at this point. Stac a' Phris (233472) has a large natural arch that can easily be viewed from the north and is a nesting ground for kittiwakes and other gulls in late spring and early summer.
Rubha na Beirghe is a large accessible promontory containing the remains of a fortified dwelling, and further on, just inland of **Rubha Caol**, there is a deep hole where the cliffs enclose the sea. Follow the posts around **Rubha**

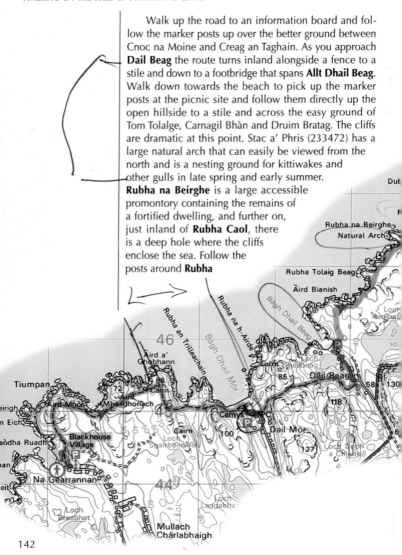

142

Neidalt, along the western shore of Loch Siaboist and across the causeway to reach the road at **Siabost bho Thuath**.

If you wish to shorten the route, this would make a good place

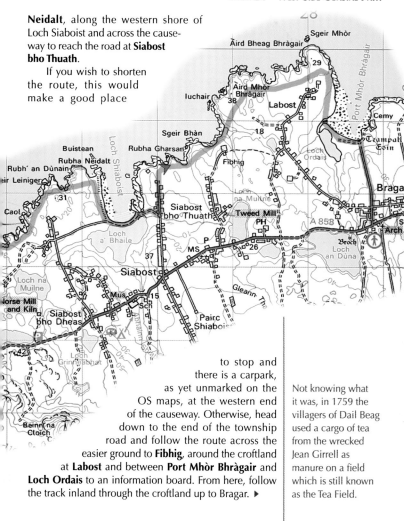

to stop and there is a carpark, as yet unmarked on the OS maps, at the western end of the causeway. Otherwise, head down to the end of the township road and follow the route across the easier ground to **Fibhig**, around the croftland at **Labost** and between **Port Mhòr Bhràgair** and **Loch Ordais** to an information board. From here, follow the track inland through the croftland up to Bragar. ▶

Not knowing what it was, in 1759 the villagers of Dail Beag used a cargo of tea from the wrecked Jean Girrell as manure on a field which is still known as the Tea Field.

143

Rubha Gruaig and Stac a' Phris, two of the many features along the cliffs

WILDFOWL AND WADERS

In recent years a small flock of white-fronted geese has overwintered on the grazings around Loch Urghag and a rare snowy owl has been seen on the moorland around Barabhas. Since Hedwig, the snowy owl in the Harry Potter books and films, brought the species to the public's notice, they have become a must-see bird. However, you will be extremely lucky to see one on a single visit.

The combination of high shingle banks and sandy shorelines backed by freshwater lochs found at Loch a'Bhaile, Loch Ordais and Loch Arnol is good for waders, particularly during their spring and autumn migration. Black-tailed godwit, curlew sandpiper, little stint, green sandpiper and greenshank can be found among the more numerous dunlin, knot, ringed plover, sanderling and redshank. Loch na Muilne (315496) is a reserve belonging to the Royal Society for the Protection of Birds with an open stone hide. During late spring it is an important breeding site for the red-necked phalarope. Being the first landfall on the eastern side of the Atlantic, storms can also result in American species, such as the lesser yellowlegs, turning up in the area.

WALK 25

Beinn Bhragair

Start/Finish	Near the road end at Pairc Shiaboist (NB267457) but avoid parking in the turning circle for buses at the end
Highest point	Beinn Bhragair 261m/856ft
Climb	400m/1300ft
Distance	10km/6 miles
Time	4hrs
Map	OS Explorer 460; OS Landranger 8
Refreshments	The Inn Between at Siabost and the Doune Braes Hotel just south of Càrlabhagh are open all year including Sundays. Otherwise opportunities for food and drink are few and far between on the west side of Lewis. The café at Gearrannan is open Mondays to Saturdays from May to September and the Morven Gallery just north of Barabhas is open Mondays to Saturdays from April through to the end of September

Although Lewis is devoid of Munros, Corbetts and Grahams with Mealaisbhal, its highest point, only attaining a modest 574m (1883ft) it does possess some wonderful little summits and Beinn Bhragair is one of them. It is a very rocky hill and stands out boldly above the surrounding heather and peat moor. As long as there has not been excessive rain, the ascent is easy and will take no more than a couple of hours, making it an ideal short route to take in when exploring other features along the north-west coast of Lewis.

The views from the summit are spectacular. To the south are the mountains of Harris and West Lewis; to the north is a vast expanse of moor and lochans with only Muirneag, the most northerly Marilyn, breaking the horizon and out to the west there is the Atlantic. Other than the croft houses that string out alongside the main road and the remains of the many shielings dotted across the moor, the land remains wild.

Go through the gate at the end of the road and follow the tarmac track through the peat banks to the unoccupied buildings at the end. Passing the buildings on the left brings you to Airigh Nupe (262434) where there are the remains of a shieling, unmarked on the Landranger map. Climb the obvious grassy slope behind the shieling to the skyline then, once on the plateau, bear left to the trig point and summit cairn. Despite its modest height, **Beinn Bhragair** provides impressive views, not least of the sharp divide between the fertile coastal strip and the central peat moor.

For a shorter walk you can retrace your steps and return to the road along the track, but to explore the many shielings around the foot of Beinn Bhragair and its neighbours first descend the southern slopes of Beinn

Beinn Bhragair from Siabost

Bhragair to find Gearraidh Mhàolan (267428). Continue over the summit of **Beinn Rathacleit** to Gearraidh Rahacleit (260420), then head east to Uishal (266418) and unnamed shielings to the south of **Beinn Feusag** before turning north-east to **Gearraidh Choinnich**.

Climb **Beinn Choinnich** if you wish; otherwise slip through **Gleann an t-Srath**, crossing the stream to visit a final shieling site at Gearraidh an t-Srath (277442), and then pick up the west bank of Feadan Bealach nam Buaim – a big name for a small stream. This leads to a ford (271445) and a track that will bring you back through some gates to the road end. If in doubt, head west to pick up the tarmac track, although you may find it involves striding across a number of muddy streams.

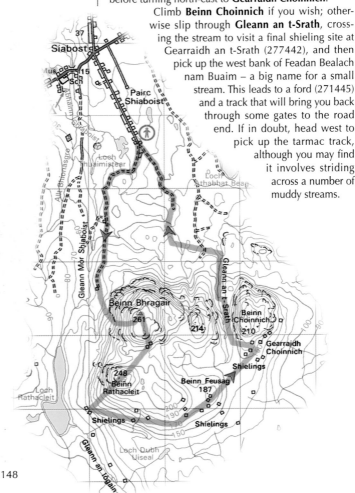

148

FUEL FOR FREE

Increases in the price of heating oil have led many islanders to start using peat again, and in 2008 the Stornoway blacksmith experienced an upsurge in demand for the traditional peat iron (*tosg*), which varies in design depending on the nature of the local peat.

Although peat is a free fuel, cutting it and getting it home is hard work. Starting in May, the peat bank is first cleared of heather turf so that the exposed peat can be cut and thrown onto the bank to dry – a task most easily done by two people working in tandem. Once stacked and thoroughly dry, the peats are carted home and built into a large stack with a greabhadh – an outer retaining wall with alternate layers of peats leaned to form a distinctive herring bone pattern. A croft can burn as many as 15,000–18,000 peats in a year and as it takes a practised hand to cut more than a 1000 peats a day, it is a major undertaking to get in the annual requirement. People employed outside the croft cannot always find the time required and tend to rely on more convenient fuels, but with high energy prices looking set to stay, increasingly islanders may be spending their weekends on the peat banks.

Looking north from the summit of Beinn Bhragair

Looking back towards the Butt of Lewis lighthouse

WALK 26
Around the Butt of Lewis

Start/Finish	Butt of Lewis Lighthouse (NB520664)
Highest point	Along the cliffs 40m/131ft
Climb	113m/370ft
Distance	11km/7 miles
Time	3–3½hrs
Map	OS Explorer 460; OS Landranger 8
Refreshments	The tea rooms at Eòropaidh can be included in the walk but refreshments can also be found at Café Sonas at the Port of Ness, The Cross Inn at Cros and Borve House Hotel at Borve

A few years ago *The Guinness Book of Records* claimed that the Butt of Lewis was the windiest spot in the UK. Other locations make similar claims, but being on the exposed north-west tip of Lewis with persistent battering from the Atlantic winds, this walk around the Butt of Lewis is certainly best left for a calmer and preferably sun-blessed day. Then you are more likely to feel at ease walking along the exposed cliff tops with the sea boiling below – and more willing to bide your time to take in the birdlife and ponder on the prehistory around you.

The red-brick Butt of Lewis lighthouse was built by brothers David and Thomas Stevenson in 1862 and remains an important beacon for shipping. Today the lighthouse acts as the monitoring station for the automatic lights on the Flannan Isles, North Rona and Sula Sgeir and is the radio control station for the North Minch area. The light itself was automated on 30th March 1998 and is now remotely monitored from the Northern Lighthouse Board's headquarters in Edinburgh. The brothers were of the third generation of the famous Stevenson family who designed and built 97 lighthouses around the Scottish coastline over a span of 126 years that ended in 1937. Thomas's son, Robert Louis Stevenson, was a great disappointment to his father in that he chose not to enter the family profession, instead finding fame as the author of classics including *Treasure Island* and *Dr Jekyll and Mr Hyde*.

Kittiwakes, fulmars and shags nest along these cliffs and there is always something to watch.

Start from the lighthouse and follow the cliffs south-west, keeping at a safe distance from the very edge of the cliff top, which is prone to collapse. However, stay near enough to enjoy the wheeling birdlife below. ◄ Further out to sea, gannets will be riding the winds and diving for fish and there is always the prospect of seals, porpoise and possibly a basking shark.

After about 1km, at the point where the coastline turns due west to a promontory, there is a noticeable flat-topped, grassy rock stack called **Luchruban** or Pigmy's Isle, so named because it is alleged to have been inhabited by a race of pigmy people. The small bones found there turned out to be the remains of birds and mammals, which probably formed part of the diet of the early Christian who occupied the stone cell on the summit. This tidal island is a piece of the original cliff which has been separated by the continual erosion of the pounding sea. At low tide it is possible to descend a scree gulley and climb the rocky wall of the island.

Luchruban (Pigmy's Isle) is the grassy, flat-topped rock in the middle distance

The remains of the cell can still be seen, facing north-east away from the prevailing wind and back along the riven cliffs towards the Butt. Make sure you keep an eye on the tide and don't stay too long otherwise you could be experiencing the hermitic life yourself until the next low water in 12hrs' time.

Either circumnavigate the promontory above the natural sea arch of **Roinn a' Roidh**, 'Eye of the Needle', which is better seen from much further south, or head due south to **Cunndal** and then south-west towards the skerries at **Sìnntean**, following the marker posts and passing through a couple of gates to reach the relative shelter on the

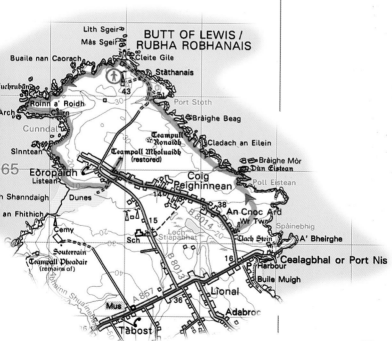

beach of **Tràigh Shanndaigh**. When you are ready to continue, head east to the back of the dunes and follow a track that leads up to the township of **Eòropaidh**, crossing the B8013 twice until at the end of a flower-strewn path of buttercups, you arrive at **Teampall Mholuaidh**, St. Molveg's Church.

TEAMPALL MHOLUAIDH

This tiny church dates from sometime between the 12th and 14th centuries and was once one of the three main centres of Christianity in the Outer Hebrides. It is recorded as being a centre for pilgrimage in the 16th century when the sick and infirm came here seeking miraculous cures for ailments, sores and insanity. The church was extensively restored in 1912 and is still used for a monthly service in all but the coldest months. It is stuck out behind the croft houses amid the narrow field strips. When it came to apportioning land for crofting it was not a priority to be generous with space around the chapel and it is tightly confined within a stone wall. Perhaps this was because the chapel stood for the wrong type of religion; perhaps because conditions were such that every available piece of productive land needed to be used. Whatever the reason, the chapel now seems strangely out of place as though the community has turned its back on it. However the interior is charming and well worth a visit.

On returning to the road, turn left along the B8014 to An Cnoc Ard and left again on a waymarked track that leads past the twin standing stones of **Clach Stein** to **Dùn Eistean**. This is the site of a medieval fort and is accessed by crossing a steel footbridge that can be said to span the Atlantic. There are grassed-over footings of several buildings that excavation has shown to include dwellings, a barn and kiln for drying grain as well as a man-made pond to catch fresh water. A large oval mound at the highest point of the stack has the medieval remains of a fortified stone tower, known as *Taigh nan Arm* (the Armoury) and associated with the Clan Morrison; recent finds of musket balls and pistol shot are thought to date back to 1595-96 when they were besieged by the MacKenzies.

To return to the lighthouse, head north-west along the back of the crofts, perhaps stopping off at the beach at **Port Stoth** for a paddle to refresh tired feet.

GOURMET GUGA

The Gaelic name for gannet chicks is *guga*, and the people of Ness (Nis), the Niseachs, are licensed to kill several thousand of them each year. They do this with the consent of both the Royal Society for the Protection of Birds and the Scottish Society for the Prevention of Cruelty to Animals, under a special dispensation dating back to the 1954 Protection of Birds Act under which gannets were designated a protected species. Every year the hunters go and stay on Sula Sgeir, a rocky outcrop about 1km long and 150m wide located 42 miles out to sea to the north of the Butt of Lewis. Sula Sgeir means 'Solan Skerry', solan or solan goose being an alternative name for the gannet. It is a pretty wild and stormy place with rough seas and strong winds. A report written in 1797 says: 'There is in Ness a most venturous set of people who for a few years back, at the hazard of their lives, went there in an open six-oared boat without even the aid of a compass'. Even today, in a motorised vessel, the trip is no pleasure cruise.

Guga was a popular meat in earlier times in Scotland. In the 16th century it was served at the tables of Scottish kings and was a favourite with the wealthy as a 'whet' or appetiser before main meals. Guga is still regarded as a delicacy in Ness today, though for others it is an acquired taste. Every August a hardy team of Nessmen set sail for Sula Sgeir to kill around 2000 young birds, taking juveniles that remain at the nest site having been abandoned by their parents to encourage them to take flight and fend for themselves. The hunters bring home their catch about two weeks later to meet an eager crowd of customers, who snap up as many of the birds as they can. The demand is often so great that the birds have to be rationed out to ensure that each person does not go without a taste of guga.

In recent years the annual cull has been the focus of attention of bird protectionists who have tried to ban the cull completely. But tradition dies hard and the Sula Sgeir trip still goes on and the people of Ness continue to enjoy the taste of guga. It is often described as tasting somewhere between a good steak and salted mackerel. Ness folk say it's better meat than any fish they have tasted, and better fish than any meat!

OTHER SITES TO VISIT

There are other Neolithic sites to visit while in the north-west corner of Lewis that are only a short walk from the road, either side of the main road in the township of Siadar. At 4.7m, Clach an Truiseil, the 'Thrushel Stone' (NB375538), is the tallest standing stone in Scotland and would have been taller still before the peat built up around it. No-one knows what it was for. One explanation is that is was a navigation marker to help seafarers find their way to a nearby beach which is one of the few places to land on this rocky coast. There is also speculation that the stone dates back to the early Norse raiders and settlers and marks the grave of a Norse Prince who died in a nearby battle. With the story having passed into folklore, perhaps there is sufficient truth to warrant further archaeological investigation.

On the opposite side of the road, at the end of a track that curves around the south side of Loch an Dùin, is Steinacleit (NB396541), which contains the remains of either a chambered cairn or some kind of domestic settlement in the middle of a 16m oval of upright slabs. There are the remains of a dun on the island in Loch an Dùin, linked to the shore by a man-made causeway, part of which is now submerged.

WALK 27

Heritage Walk from Tolstadh to Port Nis

Start	Bail' Ur Tholastaidh (New Tolsta, NB533487)
Finish	Europie crossroads in Lìonal (NB237634)
Highest point	Druim Ghinneabhal 112m/367ft
Climb	322m/1054ft
Distance	22km/14 miles
Time	6–7hrs
Map	OS Explorer 460; OS Landranger 8
Refreshments	There is nothing en route, but various options near the finish include the tea rooms at Eòropaidh, Café Sonas at the Port of Ness, The Cross Inn at Cros and Borve House Hotel at Borve

Don't be deterred by the fact that this is a linear walk. Both Tolstadh and Port Nis are well served by buses with eight services on weekdays and five on Saturdays, but none on Sundays. Currently the W5 services depart from Stornoway bus station at 0755 and 0840 on weekdays and reaches Tolstadh within 40mins. For the return, the W1 service departs from the Europie road junction in Lìonal at 1535, 1805, 1915 and 2020 on weekdays and gets to Stornoway in just over an hour. However, schedules do change, so check the current timetables online at www.cne-siar.gov.uk/travel or pick up copies at a local tourist information point.

The 22km route will take 6–7hrs, so even allowing a generous amount of time for investigating landmarks, nature-watching and rests and relaxation, you should easily make the 1805 service from Lìonal safe in the knowledge that you still have the two later services as backstops. You can walk the route in reverse, but the bus services are not quite as conveniently timed. Alternatively, you could make arrangements with a taxi service, although this will be considerably more expensive and will not give you the opportunity to pass the time of day with fellow bus passengers. My personal preference is to get all the bus travel done at the start of the day, leaving a car at Lìonal and catching the first bus into Stornoway with a quick change to the Tolstadh bus, which wanders around the backroads picking up gregarious schoolchildren who chatter away in Gaelic and English, switching tongues every other sentence.

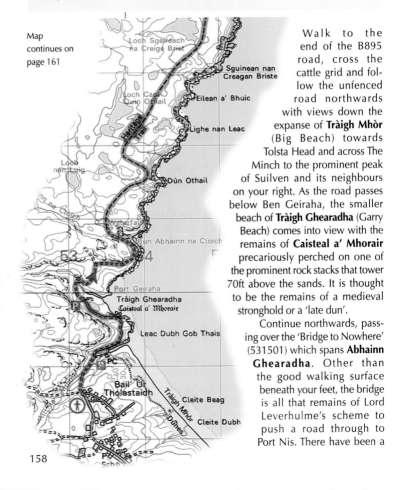

Map continues on page 161

Walk to the end of the B895 road, cross the cattle grid and follow the unfenced road northwards with views down the expanse of **Tràigh Mhòr** (Big Beach) towards Tolsta Head and across The Minch to the prominent peak of Suilven and its neighbours on your right. As the road passes below Ben Geiraha, the smaller beach of **Tràigh Ghearadha** (Garry Beach) comes into view with the remains of **Caisteal a' Mhorair** precariously perched on one of the prominent rock stacks that tower 70ft above the sands. It is thought to be the remains of a medieval stronghold or a 'late dun'.

Continue northwards, passing over the 'Bridge to Nowhere' (531501) which spans **Abhainn Ghearadha**. Other than the good walking surface beneath your feet, the bridge is all that remains of Lord Leverhulme's scheme to push a road through to Port Nis. There have been a

158

Caisteal a Mhorair

number of proposals to put a road through ever since, but clearly none has met with success. For the moment be thankful that the track exists at all because it ends abruptly at a smaller bridge across **Abhainn na Cloich** and from then on, although the path is well marked with green and yellow posts, the going gets distinctly boggy. On clear days it is probably better to follow a well-worn sheep path along the top of the cliffs which is both drier underfoot and affords better views down to the sea.

The next landmark is **Dùn Othail**, a natural fortress set nearly 200ft above sea level which is separated from the mainland by a steep ravine called Nicolson's Leap.

Legend has it that the clan chief had ordered **Nicholson** to be castrated for some heinous crime he had committed. In desperation Nicolson abducted the chief's only child and was pursued to Dùn Othail where he leapt across the chasm. Finding himself able to negotiate, he offered to surrender the child if the chief castrated himself. This done, Nicolson leapt into the sea with the child shouting, 'I shall have no heir and he shall have no heir!' A gloriously understated version of this legend was retold by Captain FWL Thomas in an article titled On the Duns of the Hebrides published in Volume 5 of Archaeologica Scotica in 1890, where he wrote, 'Several subterfuges, which are too technical to be reproduced here, were tried to deceive Mac Nicol, but in vain, and

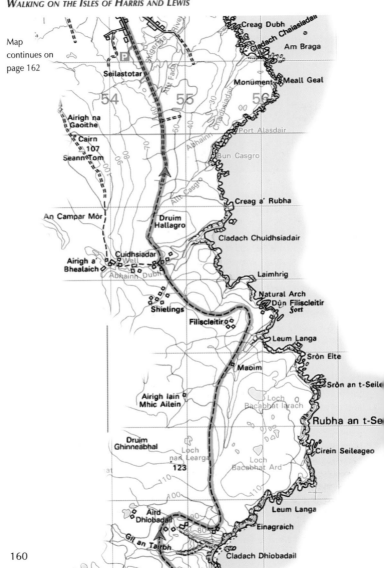

Map continues on page 162

to save the child the chief consented.' Oh, the ingenuity that must have come into the mind of man with such a choice to make! Thomas, an antiquarian, who was the first person to photograph St Kilda, notes that this legend is also found in other parts of the Hebrides.

Continuing north, the marker posts lead inland for 500m or so to the west of Loch Dubh an Toa and onwards to **Loch Sgeireach na Creige Brist** over the undulating moor. The trail goes inland again to cross Gil an Tairbh ('stream of the bull') and Gil Dhìobadail which join just before flowing into the sea at **Cladach Dhìobadail**. There are remains of shielings at both **Aird Dhìobadail** and at Lower Dibadale (554546). Leave this pleasant little valley and follow the red-capped posts that mark a short diversion to the route shown on both Explorer and Landranger OS maps. After 200m or so the routes come back together and from then on it is probably best to stick close to the main path marked by the yellow-capped posts as the ground to the east around the Bacabhat lochs and out towards Rubha an t-Seilieir, 'Cellar Head', is so up-and-down that it's tiring.

The ruins at **Maoim** are quickly reached and the ground gets easier towards **Filiscleitir**, which is perhaps the highlight of the route and good reason for walking it south to north, leaving the best bit until the end. Filiscleitir is the traditional area that people from the township of Lìonal used for their summer airidhean where the women, children and family cattle moved for the summer months to benefit from fresh moorland grass and relieve pressure on land around the croft. ▶ But the main ruin on the cliff-top is Edgemoor Hall (561576), erected as a place of worship by John Nicolson. He was born in Lìonal but emigrated to America, married and became a member of the Plymouth Brethren. When he returned to Lewis with his wealthy and very pious wife in the 1900s he built a house, called Dune Tower, on the edge of the cliff and then a chapel for the people of the airidhean. It was said that the psalm singing and the sound of the harmonium could be heard all over the moor. The couple conducted services here for many

The airidhean were traditional places for courting which resulted in many marriages between people from the Nis area and Tolstadh.

South side of Tolsta Head

The obelisk at Meall Geal (NB563607) commemorates John Wilson Dougal, an amateur geologist who in 1905 discovered what is known today as flinty-crush rock.

years with trawler crews from Buchan landing to take part in Sunday services. By the 1930s it was all over; John Wilson Dougal recorded spending a night in the then deserted Dune Tower in his memoirs published posthumously in 1937. ◀

Following the marker posts soon leads to a gravelled track which was built by people of the townships themselves well before Leverhulme proposed a road from Nis to Tolstadh and appears on OS maps from the middle of the 18th century. The summer shielings, caravans and the repurposed bus along the banks of Abhainn Dubh at **Cuidhsiadar** show that some local people are still coming out to enjoy the moor during the summer months just as their ancestors did, and being resourceful Hebridean they will make best use of whatever is at hand. Continue towards the road end at **Sgiogarstaigh** and onwards to your final destination.

LEVERHULME AND THE LONG ISLAND

Lord Leverhulme bought Lewis in 1918 and immediately initiated and personally funded a series of ambitious schemes designed to transform it into a vibrant economy based on fishing and chemicals. But faced with a population whose steadfast desire to be self-sufficient subsistence crofters was stronger than his drive to turn them into waged factory workers, his plans came to nothing. In 1923 when he abandoned Lewis to concentrate on Harris, which he had bought in 1919, he offered the land to the populace to be held in local trusts. Only the town of Stornoway took up the offer and established the Stornoway Trust to administer the land. The Trust was a unique institution until fairly recently when other highland and island communities, such as the North Harris Trust, have taken land into communal ownership.

When he died in 1925 Lord Leverhulme's estate quickly sold off both Harris and the rest of Lewis at knock down prices. It is easy to point to the relics and follies that mark his time here, such as the Bridge to Nowhere, and silently gloat. But while he may not have shown sufficient empathy with the people whose lives he wanted to change, the islanders may have been better off by embracing some of Leverhulme's ideas. He was adamant that small-scale crofting would not result in widespread prosperity and, for the most part, history has proved him right.

TOLSTA HEAD WALK

Starting at Cnoc a' Runaire (Camach Park, NB542467), behind a row of bungalows, you can follow a series of numbered marker posts around Tolsta Head. This walk has stunning coastal scenery with high cliffs, sea stacks and a number of natural arches. The plant life is rich and varied and you are sure to see many species of birds, including skua which congregate on the grassland in early summer to raid the nests of the kittiwakes and herring gulls. Seals often bask at the foot of the high cliffs and dolphins, porpoises and occasionally whales can be seen close to shore, so pack your binoculars. To provide time for wildlife watching, allow 3hrs.

WALK 28

*A walk to the tidal island
of Eilean Chaluim Chille*

Start/Finish	In the village of Cromor, parking somewhere near the public telephone (NB399213)
Highest point	Creag Mhòr 33m/108ft
Climb	240m/790ft
Distance	7km/4½ miles
Time	2–3hrs
Map	OS Explorer 457; OS Landranger 14
Refreshments	The Loch Erisort Inn on the main road into the Lochs district is open all year

The north-east corner of the Lochs area of Lewis is undeniably picturesque and well worth exploring. Although not far from Stornoway as the crow flies, the area still feels remote and was once more easily reached by sea than by road. Despite being devoid of significant hills, the headland between Loch Èireasort and Loch Odhairn is surprisingly rough and wild with rocky outcrops, gullies and cliffs and excellent views of the many uninhabited islands. Many of the summits of the modest hills near the coast are topped with marker cairns, used both to guide boats safely home through the offshore reefs and to act as markers for fishing grounds. Until well into the last century, fishing was the main industry and staple diet in the area with Cromor being home to a fleet of nearly 30 boats.

There is a 7km way-marked walk that starts and finishes at Cromor and takes in the tidal island of Eilean Orasaidh to the east of the village. But if you are at all interested in history you should take this walk to the tidal island of Eilean Chaluim Chille to the west of the village where there are the ruins of a church dedicated to St Columba who died on Iona in 597AD. A church is thought to have been founded here about 800AD and it became an important centre of religion, being cited in a report of 1549 as the main place of worship for the parish of Lochs. The cemetery was in use until 1878, so the mourners would have to make the crossing while the tide was ebbing to ensure that the proceedings were completed before the rising tide cut off their retreat back to the mainland. You will need to do the same! Check the time of low water on the day you plan your visit at a tourist information office, by contacting the Stornoway coastguard (01851 702688) or on the BBC weather website (www. bbc.co.uk/weather/coast/tides) and then plan your walk to arrive at the cross point at Crobeag 2hrs before low water and ensure you are ready to walk back along the causeway no more than 2hrs after low water. Note that tide tables always list times as Greenwich Mean Time, (GMT) and you may need to add an hour for British Summer Time (BST). As this walk is not long, it can be combined with Route 29 to the deserted village of Stiomrabhaigh to make a full day out in the South Lochs area, ordering them according to the time of low water.

From **Cromor** head off west, taking the right-hand fork to **Crobeag** and continue down to the causeway. Once across, a path leads left to the ruins of the church marked **Eaglais Chaluim Chille**. In late spring the area around the ruins is a mass of yellow flag irises. ▶ Just beyond the ruins is a remarkable cairn that looks like a piece of modern 'land art'. It is certainly man-made with smaller stones wedged in to balance the precarious larger rocks.

The many graves scattered among the ruins are worthy of investigation as some of the headstones remain legible.

Piled rocks on Eilean Chaluim Chille

Continuing the tour of the island in a clockwise direction, there are fine views west down Loch Èireasort and across to the township of Ceòs. However, the going is difficult as there are no footpaths and the heather can be knee-high, so it is best to keep to the higher ground. Head north up the west side keeping the shoreline on your left and the summit of Creag Mhor (384216) and then Loch na Cartach and Loch na Muilne on your right, to bring you to the north side of the island where a small peninsula leads to the island of Crois Eilean. It is an easy scramble across the exposed rocks to reach the cairn at its summit and the views north-east up to the Aird Raerinis and Eye peninsulas certainly make it worth it. But don't linger too long before heading down the east coast to make the crossing back to Crobeag before the tide returns and swamps the causeway.

EILEAN CHALUIM CHILLE – THE GARDEN OF LEWIS

It is considered likely that the interests of the church on Eilean Chaluim Chille spread across to the Crobeag mainland and beyond. The secluded ruins on the shore near Meall na Eoin may have been a priest's house, and there was a walled garden on Croft No 5 in Cromor known locally as 'Leis-an Theambuill',

Tidal crossing to Crois Eilean with a view across Loch Èireasort

167

the 'Garden of the Temple', although the stones were removed for use elsewhere at the end of the 19th century. The Columban monks were self-sufficient and are thought to have grown vegetables, fruit and crops, and possibly made use of an old Norse mill on the stream at Torasdaidh on the mainland. There would have been an ample supply of fish in the loch, yet the monks introduced grey mullet into Loch nam Bodach, a freshwater loch on the other side of the village, and they can still be found there today.

There is evidence that the Macleods, who held Lewis for a few hundred years prior to 1610, took over Eilean Chaluim Chille when the monks abandoned it and continued to use it as a granary, orchard and market garden, shipping produce by sea to the old castle in Stornoway. The island remained a prised possession of many subsequent owners. Today it is rare to see vegetables, yet alone fruit, being grown anywhere on Lewis or Harris. However, there is a resurgence of committed horticulturists prepared to face up to the challenges. The most obvious challenge is the persistent wind, which scorches young plants. There are various ways of providing windbreaks: traditional stone walling; hedging with quick-growing species such as willow; or using poly-tunnels. The residents of the old blackhouses used to build 'planticrues', which were small walled gardens next to their houses, just the right size for a vegetable patch.

Other challenges are the acidity of the soil, which needs to be neutralised with sand or seaweed, and the wet and boggy growing conditions which call for good drainage to be put in place. If you can get all that right, all that remains is dealing with the midges which can severely detract from the pleasure of gardening. The only way to cope is to wear a midge net and long sleeves and to use plenty of insect repellent. Given the problems they had to overcome, the achievements of the St Columban monks deserve our respect.

WALK 29

The deserted village of Stiomrabhaigh

Start/Finish	Park in the village of Orasaigh, just after the cattle grid (NB362118)
Highest point	Giearol 77m/252ft
Climb	192m/630ft
Distance	4km/2½ miles
Time	1–2hrs
Map	OS Explorer 457; OS Landranger 14
Refreshments	The Loch Erisort Inn on the main road into the Lochs district is open all year

The South Lochs and Pairc area of south-east Lewis is one of the most remote and sparsely populated regions of the UK with a population of little more than 400. Yet this was not always the case. Until the 19th century there were in excess of 30 townships scattered along the sea lochs and around the coast. Getting to many of them on foot would be a major undertaking. Thankfully it is possible to sample the remoteness of these lost townships by visiting Stiomrabhaigh which is less than 2km from the nearest road.

From **Orasaigh** climb the wooden steps near the cattle grid up the hillside and through a kissing gate to the first marker post. Follow the way-marked trail to the eastern shore of **Loch Shaghachain** and across the open moor towards Loch Sealg before descending westwards to the side of **Tob Stiomrabhaig** where you will find the remains of the village. It is not difficult to see why people wished to settle with shelter from the westerly wind, fertile land and a safe natural anchorage. It would make a delightful spot for wild camping. Return by the same route.

The census of 1851 shows that **Stiomarabhaigh** consisted of 16 dwellings with a population of 81. By 1858 there were none. Clearances had been well

169

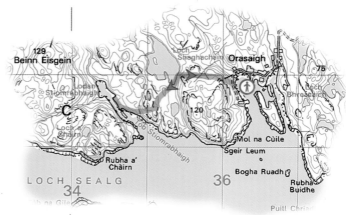

underway in the area during
the first half of the 19th century;
many of them brutal and uncaring. The residents of
Stiomrabhaigh were better placed than most in that
they leased their crofts directly from the land-owner.
However, when the leases expired they accepted an
offer of crofts in Leumrabhagh to the east. Lewis was
relatively prosperous right up until World War I, which
put an end to the herring trade with Russia and Eastern
Europe. In spite of the clearances the remaining population still increased, putting pressure on land. There

Looking down Tob Stiomrabhaigh to Mullach nan Ron

were numerous requests to resettle Stiomrabhaigh, all of which were resisted by the landowners, and it was not until 1921 when Lord Leverhulme abandoned his ambitious plan for Lewis that crofters returned to the township. Even the resettlement was marked with tragedy as two young men were drowned while transporting household goods from Calbost. These settlers were never officially recognised as crofters by the government; they received no help and no road was built to the township. Given the difficulties of living without facilities, over the next 20 years a number of the families drifted back to Leumrabhagh. At the start of World War II only two families remained, and by the end of the 1940s Stiomrabhaigh was once again deserted. Today there is much of the township to be seen; its ruined buildings, lazybeds and field walls stand in splendid isolation between the moor and the sea.

EVACUATED VILLAGES OF LOCHS AND PAIRC

To get some idea of how densely the region was once populated, it makes an interesting exercise to plot the known evacuated villages on the map. Most of them are on the coast or on a sea loch, so there must have been a fair amount of sea-borne traffic between them and the larger centres of population. In the hinterland behind many of these villages the map shows 'airigh' indicating the presence of summer shielings. This suggests that many of these settlements were sufficiently well populated to make it necessary to seek out whatever grazing was available during the summer months.

The original Pairc Sheep Farm that was responsible for the majority of clearances in the area started in Bhalamus about 1802 and systematically swept people from the land for over half a century as it expanded northwards, ending with Stiomrabhaig in 1857. Traditionally the landlords and their factors are cast as the villains. However, many landlords were in severe financial difficulties themselves and were faced with a large and rapidly growing population that was increasingly unable to support itself due to regular crop failures and slowly declining yields. Lewis became notorious for poverty, squalor and vulnerability and records show that in 1817 alone the financially stressed Earl of Seaforth spent £6000 on grain relief for hungry tenants and squatters, many tenants having illegally subdivided their plots

Hills of north Pairc from across Loch Bhaltois on the main Stornoway to Tarbert road

for their families. Although there was undoubted sadness at leaving family and friends for good, many crofters readily grasped the opportunity to carve out a new life abroad and willingly took up the offer of a free passage to a new country; the irony being that often one of their first challenges was displacing the indigenous population they found there.

Although by no means exhaustive, the following list matches names of cleared townships with places marked on the OS Explorer maps:

Chuiriseal – NB413113
Stiomrabhaig – NB346116
Gearraidh Riasaidh – NB315110
Ceann Loch Shealg – NB294107
Budhanais – NB332100
Eilean Liubhaird – NB380100
Ailltinis – NB368088
Mol Chada Gearraidh – NB367066
Mol Truisg – NB359056
Ceann Chrionaig – NB311055
Bhrolluim – NB322031
Bhalamuis Bhig – NB291010
Bhalamuis – NB298016
Smuaisibhigh – NB273049

Gleann Claidh – N253066
Bun Chorcabhaig – NB263033
Bagh Reimseabhàigh – NB258025
Bàgh Ciarach – NB251022
Ceann Mòr – NB223067
Gil Mhic Phaic – NB217083
Sgaladal Bheag – NB220100
Sgaladal Mhòir – NB218120
Rias – NB225129
Bruinagil – NB277159
Ceann Shìphoirt – NB295163
Sildinis – NB280198
Chleiter – NB288198

For more information on the social history of Lochs and Pairc, the Museum at Gravir contains historical items, and the Ravenspoint Centre at Kershader houses the Angus Macleod Archive (www.angusmacleodarchive.org.uk) and is the home of the Pairc Historical Society.

WALK 30
Beinn Mhòr

Start/Finish	Park on a gravelled area on the right just before the road end at Eisgein (NB325123)
Highest point	Beinn Mhòr 572m/1877ft
Climb	900m/2950ft
Distance	20km/12.5 miles
Time	8hrs
Map	OS Explorer 457; OS Landranger 14
Refreshments	Only what you bring with you! This is wild country

The map suggests that the Pairc district of South East Lewis is virtually an island cut off by streams that form a continuous flow of water between the heads of Loch Sìophort and Loch Odhairn. It might as well be, as this is wild inaccessible country. It may not remain a wilderness for long though. Planning permission has already been granted for a 13-mast wind farm on the western slopes of Feiriosbhal and Beinn Mheadhanach and if an undersea cable is ever laid to transfer the electricity generated on Lewis to the nation gird, then more could follow. So enjoy these hills before the skyline is broken by masts and the quiet glens are riven by the roadways needed to erect them and access them for maintenance.

This route ascends Beinn Mhòr, the highest peak in Pairc. Despite making the maximum use of the best paths, the route still involves crossing rough and typically very wet ground as well as a number of streams, so it will be an achievement if you manage to end the day with dry feet. But it is worth doing as the views south into Pairc and west, over Loch Sìophort to the Harris Hills, are excellent. Then, as an additional bonus, there is the wildlife. Pairc has large population of red deer and they will be watching from some high ridge, even if you don't see them. Being wild country, there is a good chance of seeing a golden eagle and perhaps even a white-tailed sea eagle. The path alongside Loch Sealg also provides a balcony view of anything out in the loch, so look out for great northern diver, red-throated diver and any inquisitive seals.

Beinn Mhor, Eilean Shìophort, Caiteseal and Tòdun from Liuthaid (Walk 9)

Walk down the road to the lodge gate, bear left along a gravelled path beside metal railings and pass through a small gate that leads into the estate property. Walk around past the nursery and towards the front of the lodge and take a rising path on the

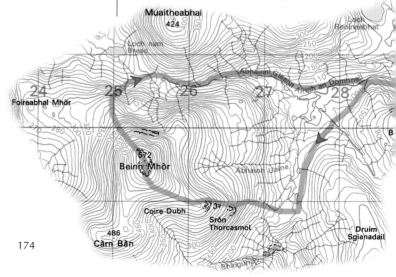

right between the front lawns to a kissing gate. This track leads down the west side of **Tòb Eisgein** and high along the north shore of Loch Shealg to **Ceann Loch Shealg**. Enjoy it, as it is the best path on the route, and please ensure the gate in the deer fence is fastened securely.

The wreck of a small craft can be seen at the head of the loch. ▶ On the south bank is the deserted township of **Ceann Loch Shealg**, cleared in the middle of the 19th century and thought to have included an inn or some kind of drinking place. Ceann Loch Shealg would have been a major hub for travellers going to and from the many villages in Park and one can imagine the inn as a forerunner of today's motorway services – somewhere where a weary walker could get shelter, food and a dram.

Cross **Abhainn Gleann Airighean Dhòmhnaill** on a good footbridge that spans the falls, walk south for about 200m and follow the gravelled stalkers' path westwards below **Beannan Mòr**. Keep left at a junction

The small island in the mouth of the river is called Dun Mhic Phi, thought to have been the home of a notorious outlaw called MacPhail.

and follow the path around into Braigh an Fhorsa until it abruptly ends, just short of a weather vane that has a metal fish as the indicator, there presumably for deer stalkers to read the direction of the wind so that they can stay downwind of their quarry.

Battle on over the rough terrain to reach the bealach at the head of **Braigh an Fhorsa** (NB275088). Coming to this spot may seem to be an unnecessary diversion, but it avoids the numerous lochans and streams that flow through Braigh an Fhorsa, reducing, but by no means eliminating, the chances of wet feet, and it gives fine views to the south down Gleann Lacasdail and across Loch Claidh. Head west and climb up to **Sròn Thorcasmol**, keeping to the ridge as much as possible as the ground either side is very damp. ◄ The ridge eases until the final 200m ascent to the rock-strewn summit of **Beinn Mhòr**. Few people would rank this modest hill among their favourites; putting it frankly, it is a featureless lump. Yet the views it affords are unparalleled, particularly westwards across Loch Sìophort and along the Harris Hills.

Descend the north-western slopes towards Loch Sìophort, skirting to the west of Creag Mhoilasail (252102), then head north to reach the **lochan** at the bealach between Beinn Mhòr and Muaitheabhal.

The OS Explorer series shows an old path running through the bealach, but it quickly becomes indistinct as you head back towards Ceann Loch Shealg and it is best

Abhainn Uaine, the 'green river', which drains the eastern slopes of Beinn Mhòr, must surely have been named because it runs all across the grassy hillside making it unpleasant walking.

Stepping up into ruins of a shieling at Airighean Dhòmhnaill

to keep to higher and drier ground on the northern side of Abhainn Gleann Airighean Dhòmhnaill, past Airighean Dhòmhnaill to reach a footbridge at NB282106. Once you have regained the gravelled path, follow it to Ceann Loch Shealg and the footbridge that leads back to the path along the north side of the loch and back to the start. If you come to a set of concrete steps, you've gone too far!

MUAITHEABHAL AND BEINN NA H-UAMHA

If you have the stamina, rather than return through Gleann Airigh an Dhòmhnaill, you could climb to the summit of Muaitheabhal, and then follow the ridge first north-east to the cairned summit of Beinn na h-Uamha and then south-east to a second cairn on a minor summit, before descending south-east into Gleann Airigh an Dhòmhnaill to regain the path to Ceann Loch Shealg.

Other options
There is plenty of scope for other good walks in the hills that surround the Lochs Claidh and Bhrolluim. The area also lends itself to wild camping but, rather than face a long trek in from the north, it is easier to arrange to be dropped off and picked up by a boat operator from Tarbert.

*Folded strata in boulders of Lewisian gneiss at Port a' Tuath,
looking towards the uninhabited island of Scarp*

WALKS ON ST KILDA
AND OTHER ISLANDS

St Kilda

The islands that make up St Kilda lie 66km (41 miles) west of Harris and were inhabited until 1930. There is much to see, including the famous village 'Street' built in 1860, the many *cleitan* used for storing foodstuff and supplies and birdlife in abundance, including the world's largest gannetry with over 60,000 nesting pairs.

Each of the six islands in the group is a 'Marilyn' – a British hill of any height with a drop of at least 150m on all sides – but unless you make special arrangements it is most likely that you will only get to land on the main island of Hirta. The contours are very close and the walking is best described as 'exhilarating'. The three main hills are Conachair (426m/1395ft), Mullach Mòr (361m/1182ft) and Oisebhal (290m/950ft), most easily ascended by using the track to the radio masts on Mullach Mòr. Needless to say, on a clear day the views across to the other islands in the group are unforgettable. Both Seatrek Outer Hebrides, www.seatrek.co.uk, tel 01851 672469 or 01851 672464, and Sea Harris, www.seaharris.co.uk, tel 0776 021 6555, run trips during the summer months. See also www.kilda.org.uk.

Other Islands

Berneray

Despite being connected to North Uist by a causeway, Berneray is part of the parish of Harris. The eastern side of the island is well populated and has a shop and tea rooms, but the western side is uninhabited with 6km of white sandy beach and uninterrupted views out to the islands in the Sound and the distant Harris Hills.

The 16km circular walk around the coast can easily be done in less than five hours and if you take the early ferry across from Leverburgh and return on the last ferry, a visit to the island during fine weather makes a memorable day out. There is plenty of wildlife to see from the ferry as it weaves its way through the myriad small islands and reefs in the Sound of Harris on the one-hour crossing. As the ferry runs every day, this trip can be done on a Sunday when everything else is closed on Harris and Lewis, but do remember to take a packed lunch with you. For further information contact 08000 665 000 or see www.calmac.co.uk.

The Shiant Islands

Like those of the much more famous island of Staffa to the south of Mull, the cliffs of the Shiant Islands, (pronounced 'shant'), are composed of columnar volcanic basalt towering 150m above the sea. The reason why they are less visited is probably to do with their relative inaccessibility. Effectively the islands are the tops of mountains that run out under the sea causing furious over-falls and tidal races at certain times of the ebb and flood. The dramatic and dangerous nature of the surrounding sea is possibly why the Sound of Shiant is known in Gaelic as the 'Stream of the Blue Men', populated by weird, blue semi-humans that will clamber about your boat singing songs and reciting poems. According to the legend, unless you can continue the song or poem, the blue men sink the boat and you drown. Despite the legend, the Tourist Information Office at Tarbert will help you will find a boatman willing to run a trip and it is well worth it, especially during late spring and early summer when the puffins arrive and nest in burrows at the top of the cliffs.

The novelist Sir Compton Mackenzie purchased the islands from the Leverhulme estate in 1925 and built a small croft house there in the 1920s. But for the last 70 years the islands have been passed down from father to son for three generations in a single family. The author and publisher Nigel Nicolson bought them with an inheritance when he was an Oxford undergraduate in 1937. He passed them to his son, Adam Nicolson, as a 21st birthday present and it was Adam who raised their profile when he wrote a portrait of the islands in his book Sea Room. Adam has now passed them down to his son,

Tom, on his 21st birthday. For further information about the islands see www.shiantisles.net.

Sea Harris runs cruises from Tarbert to the Shiant Islands during the summer. Contact Seumas Morrison, seumas@seaharris.co.uk, tel 0776 021 6555.

Taransay

Forget the debacle of the BBC's 'Castaway'. Taransay is rich in history and wildlife and well worth a visit. If the weather permits, day trips are run on Mondays to Fridays during the summer months, departing form Horgabost beach (NG046970) at 0930 and returning at 1700. See www.visit-taransay.com or telephone 01859 550260. If

Taransay from Traigh Rosamul just before sunset

you want to stay longer, there is a selection of self-catering accommodation available.

Named after Saint Tarran, the island has the remains of two chapels, both near Parbeil which was the main centre of population. Traditionally, only men were buried in the graveyard of St Keith's chapel and only women in St Tarran's. In 1900 approximately 70 people lived on Taransay but by the 1960s this had dwindled to five members of a single family, and today the island is uninhabited.

During the day there is plenty of time to climb Beinn Rà (267m), visit the two duns and other historic sites and, weather permitting, enjoy the beautiful beaches.

Flannan Isles

The Flannan Isles (Na h-Eileanan Flannach), which are best remembered for the strange disappearance of the three lighthouse keepers in December 1900, lie 34km (21 miles) north-west of Gallan Head off the Atlantic coast of North Lewis. The light was only established in 1899 and it was just a year later that the three keepers disappeared; presumably swept away during a storm. No wonder it became such a famous event, encountered in many an English lesson in the famous poem by WW Gibson.

Today they are rarely visited; as the light is automated there are no permanent residents and, if you make a visit, you will be alone apart from the seabirds. The largest island, Eilean Mòr, is a mere 600m across and rises to just 88m, with only the lighthouse and the remains of St Flannan's chapel to visit. So it is a day to take the binoculars and watch the nesting birds, which include gannets, puffins, guillemots, razorbills and petrels. Seatrek Outer Hebrides runs daily trips to the Flannan Isles and other islands during the summer season: www.seatrek. co.uk, tel. 01851 672469 or 01851 672464.

Other outliers

Seatrek Outer Hebrides (details above) also runs periodic trips to North Rona and Suilisgeir.

APPENDIX 1
Route Summary Table

The outcrop above Cathadail an Ear: an obvious place for a photograph (Walk 13)

Walk		Climb (m)	Distance (km)	Time (hrs)	Page
1	Ceapabhal and Toe Head	612	14	4.5–5	38
2	Roineabhal from Roghadal	490	8	3–3.5	44
3	Coast to Coast on the Coffin Route	336	14	4.5	50
4	Beinn Dhubh	606	11	4–4.5	54
5	The Scholar's Path	316	9	2–3	58
6	Scalpay	286	9.5	3	62
7	Circuit of Tòdun from Urgha	1029	19	6	66
8	Cleit Ard	190	6	1.5–2	72
9	Liuthaid and Mullach a' Ruisg	1127	10	4	75
10	The Skeaudale Horseshoe	1022	15.5	6.5–7	78
11	An Cliseam Horseshoe from Àird a' Mhulaidh	1065	13.5	6–7	83

Walk		Climb (m)	Distance (km)	Time (hrs)	Page
12	Stulabhal, Tèileasbhal and Uisgneabhal Mòr	1400	21	8	86
13	Muladal, Ulabhal, Oireabhal and Cleiseabhal	980	16	6	90
14	Tiorga Mòr	770	16	6	94
15	Huiseabhal Mòr, Oireabhal and Huiseabhal Beag	825	14	5–6	98
16	Ceann Loch Rèasort from Loch Ròg Beag	300	18.5	5	105
17	Griomabhal, Naideabhal a Muigh and Laibheal	900	12	5	110
18	Mealaisbhal, Cracabhal and Laibheal a Tuath	1068	15	5–6	113
19	Tamanasbhal, Teinneasabhal, Tahabhal and Tarain	1020	20	7	117
20	Suaineabhal from Cairisiadar	625	8.5	5	121
21	Bhalasaigh to Bostadh on Great Bernera	273	11	3	125
22	Calanais Standing Stones	negligible	4	1–2	130
23	Dun Chàrlabhaigh and the Gearrannan Blackhouses	488	18	5–6	134
24	West Side Coastal Path	536	18	6	140
25	Beinn Bhragair	400	10	4	146
26	Around the Butt of Lewis	113	11	3–3.5	150
27	Heritage Walk between Tolstadh and Port Nis	322	22	6–7	157
28	A walk to the tidal island of Eilean Chaluim Chille	240	7	2–3	164
29	The deserted village of Stiomrabhaigh	192	4	1–2	169
30	Beinn Mhòr	900	20	8	173

APPENDIX 2
Gaelic Language

The Gaelic language is considered to be in decline. It has been estimated that three quarters of the members of a community need to speak the language in daily discourse for its use to be maintained and transmitted to children. A hundred years ago this was the case to the north and west of the Great Glen. But by the 2001 census only 3510 Gaelic speakers lived in such communities and all of them were in the Western Isles. Even in these areas, only a minority of pre-school age children was registered as speaking Gaelic, and although it has been a compulsory part of the school curriculum for a few years, it may not be many decades before it is no longer heard in shops and bars.

Common Gaelic/Norse Terms

Abhainn	river	*Ear*	east
Aird	point	*Eilean*	island
Allt	stream	*Geodha*	chasm
–aigh, –ay	island (Norse)	*Gearraidh*	shieling village
Airigh	shieling	*Glas*	grey
Bàgh	bay	*Iar*	west
Beag	small	*Lag*	hollow
Bealach	pass	*Meall*	hill
Beinn	mountain	*Mhòr, mòr*	big
–bost	farm (Norse)	*Mula, mullach*	summit
–bhal, –val	fell, hill	*–nis*	headland
Caol	strait	*Rubha*	headland
Cleit	cliff	*Sròn*	nose
Cnoc	hill	*Toabh*	side
Creag	crag	*Tom*	small hill
–dal, –dail	valley (Norse)	*Tarbert*	isthmus
Deas	south	*Tràigh*	beach
Druim	ridge	*Tuath*	north
Dubh	black	*Uamha*	cave

APPENDIX 3
Further Reading

General reading

Lewis and Harris by Francis Thompson (Pevensey, 1999) – good souvenir guide with excellent colour photography

Riddoch on the Outer Hebrides by Lesley Riddoch (Luath Press, 2007) – broadcaster Lesley Riddoch's thought-provoking commentary on the Outer Hebrides based on her cycle journey through the island chain

Seasons on Harris by David Yeadon (Harper Collins, 2006) – travel writer David Yeadon's journal of a year spent living in Harris

The Outer Hebrides – The Timeless Way by Peter Clarke (Northampton Square, 2006) – a walk through the Outer Hebrides from the Butt of Lewis to Vatersay that makes the best of the available footpaths

History and Culture

Ancient Lewis and Harris – exploring the archaeology of the Outer Hebrides by Christopher Hughes (Comhairle nan Eilean Siar, 2008) – a colourful guide to the past with clear descriptions of the main sites worth visiting

Harris in History and Legend by Bill Lawson (Birlinn Press, 2002) – detailed history of Harris and its people by resident expert Bill Lawson, who runs the Seallam Centre at Northton

Lewis in History and Legend – the West Coast by Bill Lawson (Birlinn Press, 2008) – first of two companion books planned for Lewis

The Soap Man by Roger Hutchinson (Birlinn Press, 2003) – the story of Lord Leverhulme's failed attempt to engage with the Hebrideans and transform the economy of Lewis and Harris

The Highland Clearances by Eric Richards (Birlinn Press, 2008) – cuts through the popular myths about the clearances and examines the hard facts about what actually happened

The Discovery of the Hebrides by Elisabeth Bray (Collins, 1986) – based on the documented journals of the early travellers to the Hebrides

APPENDIX 4

Marilyns on Harris, Lewis and St Kilda

Marilyns on Harris	Height (m/ft)	Grid reference
An Cliseam	799m/2621ft	NB155073
Uisgneabhal Mòr	729m/2392ft	NB120085
Tiorga Mòr	679m/2228ft	NB055115
Oireabhal	662m/2172ft	NB083099
Stulabhal	579m/1900ft	NB133122
Sgaoth Aird	559m/1834ft	NB165039
Tòdun	528m/1732ft	NB210029
Beinn Dhubh	506m1660ft	NB089006
Huiseabhal Mòr	489m/1604ft	NB022116
Roineabhal	460m/1509ft	NG042860
Bleabhal	398m/1306ft	NG030914
An Coileach	389m/1276ft	NG086927
Heileasbhal Mòr	384m/1260ft	NG073927
Ceapabhal	368m/1207ft	NF972924
Sròn Romul (Scarp)	308m/1010ft	NA968158
Greabhal	280m/919ft	NG003891
Beinn Rà (Taransay)	267m/876ft	NB034019

Marilyns on Lewis	Height (m/ft)	Grid reference
Mealaisbhal	574m/1883ft	NB022270
Beinn Mhòr	572m/1877ft	NB254095
Tahabhal	515m/1690ft	NB042263
Cracabhal	514m/1686ft	NB029253
Griomabhal	497m/1631ft	NB011220
Liuthaid	492m/1614ft	NB175136
Gormol	470m/1542ft	NB301069
Caiteseal	449m/1473ft	NB242044

Marilyns on Lewis	Height (m/ft)	Grid reference
Suaineabhal	428m/1404ft	NB078309
Muaitheabhal	424m/1391ft	NB257114
Guaineamol	406m/1332ft	NB262136
Beinn Mheadhanach	397m/1302ft	NB090236
Cearnabhal	378m/1240ft	NB186157
Uisinis	374m/1227ft	NB337056
Ciopeagal Bheag	336m/1102ft	NB247064
Feiriosbhal	326m/1070ft	NB301146
Beinn Mholach	292m/958ft	NB355387
Roineabhal	281m/922ft	NB233212
Beinn Bhragair	261m/856ft	NB266433
Conostom	256m/840ft	NB166300
Slèiteachal Mhòr	248m/814ft	NB213188
Muirneag	248m/814ft	NB479489
Coltraiseal Mòr	228m/748ft	NB158228
Eilean Shìphoirt	217m/712ft	NB207110
Forsnabhal	205m/673ft	NB061359
Beinn Bhreac	191m/627ft	NB406121
Mullach Buidhe (Shiant Isles)	160m/525ft	NG414986

Marilyns on St Kilda	Height (m/ft)	Grid reference
Conachair	430m/1411ft	NA100002
Mullach an Eilean	384m/1260ft	NA153053
Cnoc Glas	378m/1240ft	NA062016
Stac an Armin	196m/643ft	NA151064
Bioda Mor	178m/584ft	NF104973
Stac Lee	172m/564ft	NA142049

LISTING OF CICERONE GUIDES

Tour of the Queyras
Tour of the Vanoise
Trekking in the Vosges and Jura
Vanoise Ski Touring
Walking in the Auvergne
Walking in the Cathar Region
Walking in the Cevennes
Walking in the Dordogne
Walking in the Haute Savoie
  North & South
Walking in the Languedoc
Walking in the Tarentaise and
  Beaufortain Alps
Walking on Corsica

GERMANY

Germany's Romantic Road
Walking in the Bavarian Alps
Walking in the Harz Mountains
Walking the River Rhine Trail

HIMALAYA

Annapurna
Bhutan
Everest: A Trekker's Guide
Garhwal and Kumaon:
  A Trekker's and Visitor's Guide
Kangchenjunga:
  A Trekker's Guide
Langtang with Gosainkund and
  Helambu: A Trekker's Guide
Manaslu: A Trekker's Guide
The Mount Kailash Trek
Trekking in Ladakh

ICELAND & GREENLAND

Trekking in Greenland
Walking and Trekking in Iceland

IRELAND

Irish Coastal Walks
The Irish Coast to Coast Walk
The Mountains of Ireland

ITALY

Gran Paradiso
Sibillini National Park
Stelvio National Park
Shorter Walks in the Dolomites
Through the Italian Alps
Trekking in the Apennines
Trekking in the Dolomites
Via Ferratas of the Italian
  Dolomites: Vols 1 & 2
Walking in Abruzzo

Walking in Sardinia
Walking in Sicily
Walking in the Central
  Italian Alps
Walking in the Dolomites
Walking in Tuscany
Walking on the Amalfi Coast
Walking the Italian Lakes

MEDITERRANEAN

Jordan – Walks, Treks, Caves,
  Climbs and Canyons
The Ala Dag
The High Mountains of Crete
The Mountains of Greece
Treks and Climbs in Wadi Rum,
  Jordan
Walking in Malta
Western Crete

NORTH AMERICA

British Columbia
The Grand Canyon
The John Muir Trail
The Pacific Crest Trail

SOUTH AMERICA

Aconcagua and the
  Southern Andes
Torres del Paine

SCANDINAVIA

Walking in Norway

SLOVENIA, CROATIA AND
MONTENEGRO

The Julian Alps of Slovenia
The Mountains of Montenegro
Trekking in Slovenia
Walking in Croatia
Walking in Slovenia:
  The Karavanke

SPAIN AND PORTUGAL

Costa Blanca: West
Mountain Walking in
  Southern Catalunya
The Mountains of Central Spain
The Northern Caminos
Trekking through Mallorca
Walking in Madeira
Walking in Mallorca
Walking in the Algarve
Walking in the
  Cordillera Cantabrica

Walking in the Sierra Nevada
Walking on La Gomera and
  El Hierro
Walking on La Palma
Walking on Tenerife
Walks and Climbs in the
  Picos de Europa

SWITZERLAND

Alpine Pass Route
Canyoning in the Alps
Central Switzerland
The Bernese Alps
The Swiss Alps
Tour of the Jungfrau Region
Walking in the Valais
Walking in Ticino
Walks in the Engadine

TECHNIQUES

Geocaching in the UK
Indoor Climbing
Lightweight Camping
Map and Compass
Mountain Weather
Moveable Feasts
Outdoor Photography
Polar Exploration
Rock Climbing
Sport Climbing
The Book of the Bivvy
The Hillwalker's Guide
  to Mountaineering
The Hillwalker's Manual

MINI GUIDES

Avalanche!
Navigating with a GPS
Navigation
Pocket First Aid and
  Wilderness Medicine
Snow

For full information on all our
guides, and to order books
and eBooks, visit our website:
www.cicerone.co.uk.

Walking – Trekking – Mountaineering – Climbing – Cycling

Over 40 years, Cicerone have built up an outstanding collection of 300 guides, inspiring all sorts of amazing adventures.

Every guide comes from extensive exploration and research by our expert authors, all with a passion for their subjects. They are frequently praised, endorsed and used by clubs, instructors and outdoor organisations.

All our titles can now be bought as **e-books** and many as iPad and Kindle files and we will continue to make all our guides available for these and many other devices.

Our website shows any **new information** we've received since a book was published. Please do let us know if you find anything has changed, so that we can pass on the latest details. On our **website** you'll also find some great ideas and lots of information, including sample chapters, contents lists, reviews, articles and a photo gallery.

It's easy to keep in touch with what's going on at Cicerone, by getting our monthly **free e-newsletter**, which is full of offers, competitions, up-to-date information and topical articles. You can subscribe on our home page and also follow us on **Facebook** and **Twitter**, as well as our **blog**.

Cicerone – the very best guides for exploring the world.

CICERONE

2 Police Square Milnthorpe Cumbria LA7 7PY
Tel: 015395 62069 info@cicerone.co.uk
www.cicerone.co.uk